The Book
on the
Shelf of Love

M · V · T U C K

ISBN 979-8-88540-633-8 (paperback)
ISBN 979-8-88540-634-5 (digital)

Christian Faith Publishing
832 Park Avenue
Meadville, PA 16335
www.christianfaithpublishing.com

Printed in the United States of America

Preface

The Book on The Shelf of Love are recycled truths, hidden crumbs, that have fallen from past writers, Christian history overlooked and ignored. Complete at fifty thousand words, people want the truth. Five hundred years later, and here comes the reformation that Luther or Calvin never finished. Interpreting complex language of scholars, uncovering important biblical truths, truth left behind that have been erased for centuries, this is a legacy for the millennials that stands alone. Christianity, its doctrines, leaders, and their agenda plague Christians with doctrinal complexities, and with such a wealth of biblical and historical records, most Christians still do not know enough.

Like the *Left Behind* series, Tim LaHaye and Jerry B. Jenkins leave people in a misery, except this is nonfiction. Who will head this reformation? Disobedience to God is an undesirable condition that should be corrected. The Antichrist is seeking to crush Christians, God's moral law has been left behind, where men have corrupted the principles of the gospel. And the millennials they are bombarded with messages of passed-down traditions, distorted teachings, and doctrinal unity.

The disruption of those who will resist the change of reverting back to worship on Saturday will leave a mark, while the church leaders' guilty conscience will be on high alert on Sunday. I will reach

10 percent of the mainstream market share or 2 percent of the 2.2 billion Christians in the world. I've been studying the Bible since my youth, reaching the secular audience, working with book coaches and consultants, because this is my calling.

As a business owner and entrepreneur, there are many platforms that I intend to use, but preaching is my favorite. I will promote with willingness this work at every open opportunity; our eternity is at stake. The church affects the lives of the world, because the world system and laws revolve around the church, and there are over three hundred thousand Christian churches in America alone. This is real life, uncovering truth by simply telling a story. Thank you for your consideration.

Introduction

This is a revival to restore or renew life. Revival always brings in its train a richer understanding of the Scriptures. This is what it means to be inspired. This is what a God-breathed document reads like. We are on a pilgrimage looking for further revelation of truth, which lay ahead as we walk in obedience to truth already received. The spirit of truth is the Holy Spirit.

The root of the problem with restoration is not a lack of will, but for most Christians, it is the lack of knowledge. The ultimate purpose of God is to restore the church to its original condition as portrayed in the new testament—to have the right worship of God and discipline of Christ established in the church according to the simplicity of the gospel without the mixture of men's inventions. Refrain from evil thinking; this is what the reformation sought to reform.

It is true that the reformers were limited by what they knew. Lutherans cannot go beyond what Luther saw, and Calvinists they stick where Calvin left them. God had not revealed His whole will to them, and it left them in a misery much to be lamented. The reformed church has come to a period of standstill and will go no further than the instruments of their reformation.

Now we are swept away by every wind of doctrine, what is this mess the shepherds feed us, they lead us, yet we are filled with emptiness. Our cup runneth over with bitterness. Truth is perfect, but with its pleasures of knowing brings pain.

This is revival that is not wrapped into a theological principle and still addresses the issues. God will have all men to be saved and to come unto the knowledge of the truth. It is God's will to pour out His spirit upon all flesh, so let us go where inspiration leads us. This is that sound that we are listening for; here is the voice of God, now read with the eyes of faith. The word that comes from the Lord does not ask questions but makes a declaration.

This is a deep dark revelation, and this is our history. It is real and it is authentic, so give glory to God. It is His work. If you believe that there is one God and one mediator between God and man, then read the most controversial religious literature which far outweighs propagation that preys on Christian intelligence instead of drawing men to Christ.

There is little room to be original or have something significant to say with all the Christian literature over the centuries in circulation. What could possibly be said differently from every other writer in the world that would make a person read and listen, but when God speaks it resounds through every page? God kills and gives life, yet by the same stroke God uses mysterious words, and they are a death blow to all that we are. For the mysteries of God destroys our physical senses and our intellectuality.

World, what a waste to tear down all that we are, to build a sham, an imitation to devour God's perfect wisdom. Nation to nation and city to city, one by one a church decree that has changed endlessly. Never wrong, unfailing, infallible, faith falls from the Roman guards who are sleeping, who rule their sphere as other gods rule theirs, instead of pure living waters, foul waters, a dark stream black from its source of despair.

Nevertheless, the darker the mystery, the more we are illuminated by it. Only God can do a new thing and bring forth treasures from His storehouse both new and old. Plain language of everyday use, simple common words with a passive tone, so that we are without excuse. Because there is no excuse for a person who can read, and there is no difference from a person who can't read and a person who does not read and stretch their intellect toward God.

Try the spirits whether they are of God. He that knows God hears, so we must listen to God. We are exhorted to take heed to what we receive for truth, examine it, compare it, and weigh it with other scriptures of truth before we receive it. For it is not possible that the Christian world can come so recently out of such thick darkness to reach full perfection of knowledge all at once. We must look at these things as having been given a supernatural character by God in these latter times.

Most Christians share the same information. Nothing new is being revealed because what is to be known, people do not know, being intellectually ignorant. God does not give us more until we appreciate what He has already given to us. We do not receive because it is the glory of God to conceal a thing, and we must search out the matter. And it is our duty to search for truth, because some have been poisoned by the tale of time and are not innocent of ignorance. The passing of age makes a brave mind. This hurts, some courses lead straight to hell. Do not be resentful and lie in this ditch. Hear a heart that pours out a rich bitter pitch. Watch what I say for the souls that swallow hell and would have us to follow.

Writing for God is recording the words of God being the instrument turned ever so slightly as the spirit would, whether people like them or not. It is better to obey God than to find favor with man. Being a recorder for God is not retelling biblical stories, nor fantasizing, but unfolding, interpreting, expounding, and being receptive at every hiss of the Holy Spirit. This is a real reformation with instructions on righteous living. This will remove the false understanding about Christianity.

Fix your vision in the thick of Rome, keep silent and bow down, hear a message from the throne. We enter the enemy's territory with arrogance, the intellect of sound understanding, the beast and shepherds frown. They hear His Holy tone, unchallenged and unwelcomed.

Howling winds and swaying trees are praising God, as He is passing by; a quick intense thunder shower pours heavy rain. But if the clouds gather, and darkness covers all, and it releases no rain to be seen, or it doesn't produce a downpour, then consider the moment. Then the wind passes, the storm ceases, the skies clear, and the sun begins to shine. Every appearance of a rainstorm that never produces rain. Know that God is passing by bringing heavy spiritual rains. Feel the invisible rain poured on the souls of those who are watching Him pass by. If we reach out and stretch our intellect toward God, we will be drenched by the heavy rain showers that we do not see. They are spiritual rains poured into our hearts.

Rude and brutal thoughts about the substance of our life that we waste through life's journey, from the flame crucified as we travel through this world with persistence and little hope on the straight road with the blind leading us into a pit with no rope or resistance. We go astray like waters that go over our heads in haste; throwing away is wasting, wasting by gambling our substance of life until there is nothing left, not even ignorance, to the wind that passes away and comes not again. On the cleft is the short mortal life perched, not so much as frightening as division in the church.

There is a great difference between the wisdom of an illuminated man and the knowledge of a learned and studious scholar. Far more noble is this learning from God which flows from above than that which labor is acquired through academics. The Roman Empire rest on the Roman Catholic in the West, but her gaze lies at the bottom of hell, going through darkness to get to the light. Never a lower standard of meditating good and evil when it has reached the fullness of night.

Understand how to find God behind all of this, as Moses was prepared to die and of the tribe of Benjamin he said, "The Lord shall cover him all day long, and he shall dwell. between his shoulders." And Rome put Paul before the apostles. But God is a consuming fire. Wherever there is a fire, there is judgment, for a fire goes before him and after the fire tore through St. Paul's Basilica, it was rebuilt.

There is never a moment when God is not acting in an unknown but sure manner.

His immediate presence would terrify us. We are responsible for what we don't know. There is no excuse for the banished art to speak and write the abuse of life that troubled us so long ago. God uses the words and actions of others to disclose truths, which would otherwise have been hidden being well aware that anything inspired by God is far more effective than we imagine.

Always carefully gathering up the crumbs which the proud trample underfoot Everything is precious, neglecting nothing, extracting all that is useful; since this is the work of God, we must not try to justify its effect and consequences. This will vindicate itself. Ancient champions who grasp to their advantage the narrow path in earthly misery, their feet will not touch the dead dust of a hotter degree. These words sting even if the world doesn't agree. Hear the truth, understand the root, rehearse the good deeds of those that see what we see. Seal your lips and be still while we speak facts. Sinfulness stinks, salvation winks to all who surrender intact.

To know yourself as the image of God, we must live in accordance with what we are, spiritual beings. It is not only required, but it is mandatory to give priority to our inward realities. For I delight in the law of God after the inner man. Most people suppress the realization that we fail in our outward status when we don't recognize our inner man. The struggle enslaves us, and we put the conflict aside like a delusion for the success of the moment. Where outer realities rule, we never worry about being enslaved by the laws which are written on the heart of the inner man.

Deeper and deep, lower and low, turn back if not fast, do it slow. Corruption of the intellect is taking its toll. Wisdom hurried us toward the other side, to chase away the feeding crow.

Our memories are used for anything that does not outdate itself with the changing times, making forgetfulness the major cause of alienation from God. We must not forget one jot or one tittle of what God has done or what we are required to do. This generation is recklessly latched onto every distraction that the world has to offer. The vices that poison the heart have gripped the mind with twisted ideas, and we indulge in everything void of spiritual growth, never drawing closer to God.

Principles within governed by the grace of God will have us abstaining from the pleasures of this life. But we are not committed to satisfying our inner demands. Lawless shepherd's great cheats, with keys to bind and loose, while greediness tramples virtue under feet, the war required nothing but the truth, and the best observation point to the heathen practice is introduced.

We have no clue of our nature and twice as ignorant of our destiny. We don't realize that we have the same life that God has. The life which He possesses in heaven is the life that God has imparted to us here on the earth. This is a precious gift because it is for this reason that we can live a life of holiness. For it is not our own life that has been changed, but the life of God that has been imparted to us. God does not give His gifts at random, neither does He dispense them by rules. They are freely given to all. God has truly blessed us with every spiritual blessing in the heavenly places in Christ.

The corruption of the church is the conspiracy that remains from the same source of chains, those who made us to sin disturbing dust from the devil's den. The fire is on the surface. Leap higher to learn what evil has done, which is beyond a spoken word. The eternal God placed a seal on His inconceivable disgust and hatred for sin, yet we try and explain the world and give good reasons for sin. Sin is so heinous, so infamous, so revolting, so black and hellish that God dare not forgive it lightly. God is holy, and that holiness must express itself in terms of fiery indignation against the wickedness of sin. To the haughty sinner, what is left for God to do? There is nothing more that can be done for a sin-cursed race.

For God to identify Himself utterly with sin, if this does not elicit gratitude and love, then there remains no more sacrifice for sin. How can we escape the terrible finality if we neglect God's pain because of sin, His hatred of sin, His willingness to die for our sins to bring us to holiness?

The barrier stood between us and God. But the blood removes the barrier and restores man to God. Man is in favor, and God is on our side to face Satan and combat reasoning. The holy walk in newness of life is our behavior. Yet there is that something that still draws us to sin. We need the solution to the problem of our conduct and the development of our thoughts, for we must stand before God.

Unfolding the flood to yield no place for pity, arrogant souls swallowed whole in the field of blood to that Golden City. Under the shadow hiding instead of falling into the enemy hands, knocked down humbled, never gain momentum, kicked down, and stumble.

The lack of spiritual knowledge stunts our growth. We are to search for wisdom and seek after the knowledge of the truth, asking God to enlighten our eyes and opening our understanding. How can we believe what we don't know? The vantage point is history frozen and speaking, bringing a clear view to us without moving silently seeking; the will of my good master who thinks this will do us good, forty and five years escorted by angels in the name of heaven, alone and misunderstood.

We have been delivered from a power that is still present and very real, not from something that no longer exist. Sin is still here. Whosoever is begotten of God does not sit idle, inactive, not working, unprofitable, made ineffective, or put out of operation by sin.

Guidance often comes from unlikely sources like Balaam's ass. Guidance must first be identified, for it wounds and warns where it leads and play, who dare to sorrow at God's thorn; why refuse to apply wisdom before we fly away? Marching orders from a castle told us what to read, and what to do; half-truths of doom simmering in a pot of stew, of boiling glue.

Stuck in a church we walk by faith which makes every action unseen with our natural eyes. For we will not see if we are unwilling to obey. God makes us subdue self, remain silent, and submit. Reverence propels us toward silence, and silence enables us to listen. We must be humble before the mystery of God, obedient and listening. Because there is more involved than intellectual stimulation in this.

This generation is the worst generation because every evil is compiled from past generations including the distractions from this present generation. The purpose is driven by the powers and rulers of darkness of this age to mount an attack so vicious and invisible, with such an eruption of self-destructiveness, so active and yet so unnoticeable. The real drama is that this generation encourages those forces unsuspected. We drift downstream through bad faith, and changing times. Trendsetters setting the tides and we change from a lonely lake to the strength of a sweeping flood before the crisis is evident.

Such a variety of vipers bred wisdom from the Dead to the Red Sea, dust from the dearth, a curse or the final plea. Seasons are strange ahead, eat these bitter herbs and honey instead. Reasons are made plain because there are no figs on the tree, snakes became my gain, to study the wisdom shared in the den of wise men.

The stake driven in the verses yield faith falling prostrate, pull its lips, speaking in tongues, sharpen its speech, forked his horns, hissing over the stones, spitting in the dirt, into his mouth withdraws its ears from this work. The tale is strangely told to confuse the youth, cunningly kept from the old crawling along this road.

God seeks our well-being; therefore, the Scriptures was created, edited, preserved, spread, and explained by the church. Without the church, there would be no Bible. It was not handed down from heaven on a silver platter. Earthen vessels were the vehicles. The church is the medium in which the Bible grew. We do not mean to use the Scriptures as ammunition for controversy or as an act of war of words in the art of controversial differences against believers, or against the household of faith.

The church's mission to facilitate access to God's Word in a more material sense has not been accomplished, and we have perverted the nature of God's gift. We are supposed to be receptors of grace transmitting the revelation we have received from God. And our familiarity with the Bible must never become an instrument of personal power over others to coerce, judge, or punish them.

We can be sure we understand the Bible if it produces love in us. It is the book of love. It has communion as its goal, being bonded with God and our fellow neighbor. God gave us His word of hope even knowing that we would make selections unfairly from it so as to misrepresent it as we pass it from one to another.

Our intention is not to make people think that the Bible is an easy book to read. It may seem plain and no more than common sense is required to understand what is written, but that is because the guidance of the Holy Ghost is making plain the mystery of the revelation. Love for the Bible makes us want to be sure that it is really God's Word that we receive. The core interpretation is straight ahead trying to teach lost advice, from a paradise that rises above such evil, and bring the whole world to Christ.

Christianity and the church need to understand our roots. For there are many branches of Christianity, all part of the same tree. The tree has grown tall and the roots run deep, yet some branches have no leaves, they produce no fruit. The Christian church started with the Roman Catholic Church. Let us get to our roots, but not to the degree where we receive the same nutriment supply and no significant value remains for the rest of the tree.

The fathers of the church are witnesses to the early undeveloped Christianity closely related to the apostolic tradition. Therefore, all Christian believers need to know some theology but with discernment. Theory has run loose and has been allowed to take aspects of the truth to the extreme without restrains, pass the bounds of moderation. Because the root offers the fruit of their spiritual experience.

The brief voyage beneath the moon sank thousands of stars when a squall broke hard upon manhood, dark toward night reaching Mars. This work is a warning to correct the direction of Christians all over the world, to give struggling Christians a fighting chance at eternal life. I have read somewhere that we blaze a trail for ourselves, armed with the knowledge of what has come before us, and so the history of the written Word has again revealed the future.

There has been a widening of the capacity of human intelligence, but with the diminishing understanding of spiritual revelation. The superficial concept of intellectual knowledge is not enough. This book of love has a far deeper meaning than what we are able to give it alone.

Chapter 1

THE GIFTS OF THE SPIRIT

The disruption of life is a sudden change or turn of events in life's circumstances, beautiful for situation, anything that affects a settled way of life. People are set in their ways, settled in their lees. To disrupt the flow of life is most disturbing. We get comfortable where there is no comforter. The break in a pattern or routine keeps us on the edge, the ledge of uncertainty, unexpected change, and unavoidable circumstances. In the days of prosperity be joyful, but in the day of adversity we must consider that God has set the one over against the other. We all are uprooted by occurrences.

Because the earth abides forever, we try and make the earth our home. God does not want us to get comfortable here. Most people are quite comfortable and familiar with the day-to-day operations of life until tragedy strikes. In AD 70 the disciples were building the church, the temple was destroyed, and the church was scattered. What a sorrowful downfall after having made such progress. This is the first of many disruptions that the church must experience.

Generation after generation, we continue to try and get comfortable in this life. Disruption keeps God before our eyes to glorify Him in everything great or small. And so disruption in the course of life brings the world into subjection to God. Disruption learns to tell God, not man our problems believing God will solve them. Disruption of life is depressing. It dislodges and puts things out of place, agitates, and brings disturbance to familiarity.

"A time to break down and a time to build." There is an evil disease which I have seen, and it is common among men, when men try and rewrite other people's work as if their work needed correcting. Leave other men's matters alone no matter how good or noble your intentions may be. For who knows the thoughts and intents of another person's heart. Their intentions were right well, and who knows the influence God has had on that persons writing, as if it is okay to change or abridge another man's work. This is an evil disease. We have done this to the Bible, the Word of God. Whosoever despises the word shall be destroyed.

The hidden or secret books were dropped from the Bible because they were never found in any Hebrew form, but they were part of the Bible of the early church and remained so for a thousand years. Scattered here and there in the Old Testament, and now they are not printed as part of the Bible any longer. St. Jerome, in AD 400, edited the authorized Bible, but 1,100 years later, Martin Luther separated the Apocrypha in his Bible of AD 1534. The Roman Catholic Church left them scattered among the books which we include in the Old Testament. King James made the Apocrypha part of the Bible again by the hand of God, and we began to demand copies of the King James Version omitting these books, and they dropped them from the printings. The American Bible Societies took a definite stand against their publications, and they have disappeared.

Truth was placed where it seemed to belong logically or chronologically among the Hebrew books, then put together by themselves, and finally omitted. The Catholic Church reaffirmed these books as inspired. It was the reformation who made a decisive step of denying inspiration to these books of the Bible because they were not found in the Hebrew Old Testament.

This was the Reformation Anti-Christian darkness. Wandering stars who were allowed to make decisions without direct authorization from God. Thus having hindered rather than helped appreciation of the books of the Bible.

History banned, excommunicated, and this time it is not the Romans but the confusion of man. We discredit these early Bible books because we were taught to, and the Bible in part has been neglected.

We have changed the wardrobe of the past; we have changed the instrument. Thoughts have been neglected, and we have altered steps that were clearly ordered by the Lord. Iron sharpens iron, so consider the work of God: that which is crooked cannot be made straight, but God can make that straight which He has made crooked.

One generation passes away, and another generation comes and tries to alter the wardrobe of the past. If we play the drum, we are expecting to hear that drum through all eternity. If we change the instrument, we thus change men in the way they convey their thoughts. And these thoughts can easily be taken for a literal representation of the mind of God.

The steps that are clearly ordered by the Lord need not be altered. Whoever hated life more than the dead should leave their labors unto a man that shall be after them. To have rule over all their labors, and it was rightly stated that who knows if he shall be a wise man or a fool.

God does not like the word *trinity* to describe Him. They are three distinct Entities—the Father, the Son, and the Holy Ghost—but they are one. Just like the three distinct elements of the sun—the sun, the light, and the heat. We do not describe the sun as the trinity or the trinitarian sun, and it is the center of our universe. Then do not inscribe trinity to the only wise God. He is one and greater than the sun. It is inappropriate to ever compare God with the sun, but for the sake of explaining the operation of identification, it is well fitting. However, embracing the word *trinity* is offensive to God.

These are things pertaining to the kingdom of God. If you do not understand, then you do not know God on this level. This is that wisdom that strengthens the wise. Wisdom is despised, and the words are not heard when wisdom is not applied. Just as the earth revolves around the sun, our lives must revolve around God. He is the source of our being, in Him we live and move.

God does not like the word *infallible* to describe the Bible. The only way the Bible becomes infallible is if it is kept in the spiritual realm where it belongs. The moment the Bible is read without its spiritual context, it stops living and loses its harmony. The intellectual understanding behind this lies upon the way the Bible was formulated. The Bible is the Word of God that spills over into our natural world. It is the Holy Spirit that brings the Bible to spiritual life, not man.

The ironic thing is that the Jews wanted to eat the Passover. They did not want to defile themselves. So close are the doors between the visible and invisible that God let the spiritual world spill over into our natural world. We see both the spiritual and physical Passover Lamb. We glimpse behind the veil to the preparation of the Passover. They rise to kill and eat as Jesus is crucified. Understand the Bible, both natural and spiritual. God has made everything beautiful in His time.

This is that disruption of life that will shake the universe and set the world on fire. There is confusion because everyone wants to change the Bible or exchange the translation. The spirit of God is concerned about our life. The King James Version was authorized, for a man laid down his life for that translation, burned at the stakes, and Jesus was crucified on the cross. The course of religious life has been disrupted.

As another generation passes, we reap that whereon we have bestowed no labor. Other men have labored, and we have entered into their labors. We must be effective, continuing as leaders and torchbearers to keep the fire burning. Prayer warriors and Christian soldiers that can keep rank. A generation who understands the times, experts in spiritual war. Here is health to the sick and a word to the wise.

These words are spirit. Who can hear these? Moses gave us the law, and no one keeps the law because we think that Jesus kept it for us. This is the voice and judgment of this world. Wise men, who know the times, know that not obeying the commandments is not only wrong to God but also to all the people that seek to enter into the kingdom of God. We have despised the law being under grace.

This is that disruption of life that jerks us out of a comfortable relaxed position abruptly while the tides are shifting at the shock of uprooting doctrines. When we thought that we were finally settled in the truth, our understanding has been enlightened. We twist and tum from instructions like a child being chastened, but pruning hurts more so and purging is equally painful. Disruptive and disturbing to the natural course of life, cutting out dead parts, or making clean and clearing out excessive branches, yielding peaceable fruit. Correction equals expressing love. We want our fruit to remain.

When the storm is raging and the waves go over our head, the Holy Spirit, the gentle comforter, teaches us how to swim, and we swim under the water beneath the waves. We restore comfort with the fruit of our lips that create troubled seas that cannot rest. Disruption is a holy thing. It can cause a change of attitude and behavior in those who experience it.

Interpretation

To the naked eye there is no discord with ecclesiastical and apostolic tradition, but while Paul was in Rome imprisoned, the Roman Empire graciously accepted Paul's gospel. Being under grace does not void out the truth. The words of Jesus clearly have been rejected to not depart from the commandments. These are God's words, God's laws, and His commandments. For the law was given by Moses, but the grace and truth of the law came through Jesus Christ. There is a grace about the law that must be obeyed. To thrive on tolerance is not biblically sound doctrine. Our moral behavior must be transformed to the truth being expressed.

This is not written to condemn, but how can we claim to know the Father, and Son, and have no clue to the operation of the Holy Spirit? The night has come, and no man can work. The Holy Spirit is that light, but we grope in the dark. The Holy Spirit is the only one that can help us find the straight and narrow path and the only one that can teach us to walk in the narrow way. There are some strange voices in the world, and in none of them do we find pasture. The wolf scattered the sheep, and there is no shepherd. Many stumble in the night because we put out the light and hide it under grace.

As earthly vessels, we can only testify of what we have seen and heard. No man has ascended up to heaven above, or his words would be heavenly. We are earthly, not infallible. No man or woman that is of the earth, from their lips drop the infallible word. Art thou a master of divinity and knowest not these things. Check on any weak points in your faith including ignorance and enter into battle against the enemy who is fully armed.

The Sanhedrins of today still reject, abandon, and distort divine truth. Although this is not a public opinion, but the pope does not represent Christ on earth. The church has gotten it wrong more than a few times, science and chemistry, Holy Spirit and ministry; it is the appointed duty of the Holy Spirit to represent Christ on earth. The church derives its life from the Holy Spirit, and so does the Bible.

The Roman Empire, or rather the Roman Catholic Church, adopted the practices of the Sanhedrin rulers to execute punishment upon all who oppose them. To beat, murder, imprison, and burn those who had sinned. Yet while these horrific inhumane violent acts of the church have long since ceased to exist, the heart of the church has never been changed.

We overlook the Pontiff's keen insight and inside knowledge, bending the world to his will. This is always the agenda to tell us what we should think or the way he wants us to think. The mind of a brilliant politician/zero Christian. A philosopher and theologian with the limits of ecclesiastical authority. But who will take up the responsibility for refusal to accept Galileo's proof that the earth circles the sun?

The church has defiled herself with the sins of the world, and we have come to tolerate sin. To identify the Antichrist, just call the church to repentance, but the enemy will not be able to comply. There are secret sins in the heart of the church, and we are called to a change of heart. Examine the church as to what direction it is taking, because it affects the lives of the body of believers. We must discover and expose sin that need profound reform. It has indirectly infected the rest of the body at every level.

The Roman Catholic Church is the root of all Christian faith, even if our minds are darkened through ignorance. Despite differences, this is a declaration that is not up for debate. Centuries ago words written in like manner would have been banned or excommunicated. But open rebuke is better than secret love.

This is complete disruption to everything we understand to be truth. A disruption that shocks the world. The interpretation of rolling thunder, roaring from heaven, a message from the throne of God. There is only one true church, and it is not a building made by hands, but from every branch of Christianity, believers make up the bride.

Addressing the sins of the church, prayerless lives, preaching without the Holy Spirit, preaching for a price, and paying for purgatory. There is a way that seems right, but to find new balance would mean to tolerate sin. God does not tolerate sin. Men pretend to have authority to execute judgment and forgive sins, but who can forgive sins except God? Here is the danger that we must not deny, and that is the sins of the church.

Since the pontiff wants to have authority over the affairs of the church, then the same shall drink of the wine of the wrath of God without mixture. But let us not be so quick to unravel the Antichrist. Because there is a danger that lies ahead for those who are not prepared to fight. This will expose generations of error.

Many denominations are too ignorant to realize that we are all believers that are the offspring and direct result of the Roman Catholic Church. The pontiff and his hierarchy knows this and mocks our ignorance. The Roman Church pretends not to acknowledge other Christian denominations as branches of the living church, but until God calls us out, we are one big tree swaying in the wind which appears to have life but is dying from within, hollow and decayed, festering with sin.

And so this tree is full grown, its boughs reach to heaven. All the branches are full of leaves except this one branch which is at the highest point of the tree where it is barren and have no leaves. It doesn't really matter how dead or how high it may be, it is still part of the tree. An abominable branch. When the boughs thereof are withered, they shall be broken off.

God is the head of the church. The popes, they were literally rulers of kingdoms and now have begun to be seen more as spiritual leaders. Protestants have denounced Catholics as fake Christians, but little do they know that the Catholics are the root of all Christianity. Church establishments all over the world have drawn from this root of Christianity to establish their doctrine.

In fact, these are those who despise dominion, who indirectly speak evil of dignities. These speak evil of those things which they know not. These are murmurers and complainers walking after their own lust. These are raging waves and wandering stars that God has permitted, thus we see the reformation.

Recognize that we are one church and everyone is doing what is right in his own eyes. Sin at the top level makes it difficult for the church to maintain order. To maintain order would mean having some degree of control over every church in the world. But God does not allow a dead lion to have spiritual control over a living dog.

Branching off from the Roman Catholic Church, after the apostles' death, their successors were the popes and bishops who are aided by the priests. The Roman Church adopted Paul's gospel and many forms of the Sanhedrin practices. The Sanhedrins, they stoned Stephen, and Paul was consenting to his death.

The double standard that appears within the Vatican is still the same with the audacity of them to remind us of the excellence of martyrdom. Appreciate the virtue of truthfulness to bring what people say and what they do in line with this knowledge.

The pope does not represent Christ in the world as some believe, but he represents the church. The Vatican and the pope are eating and wiping the church's mouth and saying, "We have done no wickedness," who said let us take to ourselves the houses of God in possession. God detest hypocrisy. There is blood on the hands of the church, and the church sits in ruin. The structure of the church is unorganized. Our soul might be saved, but the church stands to be judged.

The root of Christianity finds its beginning in the apostolic teachings, rooted in the Roman Catholic Church. Since the Roman Church is linked so close to the founding fathers, they are supposed to be the spiritual advisors of the church. The Roman hierarchy, the moral and spiritual leaders of the world, are uniting the whole world together, but not to God.

The road is narrow, and few will be there that find it. Narrow not in the sense that there is only one branch that everyone climbs aboard and follows into eternity. Narrow not in the sense that only one church denomination has all the right answers, because it is not the only branch that follows what good is. But narrow in the sense of what we do, what we know, and how we behave. The church is fitly joined together by the hearts of people and our individual standard of moral conduct.

Our relationship with Christ is tested to see if we obey His Word, if we are concerned about what people know, or if we are withholding corn from the people who otherwise would not know the things that would bring them to the narrow path. Knowledge is the only way to apply the command to love God with all of our mind. God takes individuals whose heart are perfect toward Him and snatch them into His kingdom; they become the church.

It is more than just belief in Jesus, for the devils believe and tremble. Few be there that find the right balance and the proper structure in our daily life to keep us on one accord with the spirit of God. This is the gift of God. This is that hour we look for, and we know not what we are looking for, and how can we unless someone guides us?

The road is a behavior. To abide in Christ is a lifestyle. Understanding the gospel is not the road, but when we find out how to walk and how to behave in what we know, then we have found the straight and narrow road. One by one we are placed into God's kingdom few be there that find out that it is not about a doctrine, denomination, sect, group, or church background; none of these things will put us on the straight and narrow path.

The Christian doctrine has become so rigid and complex that most Christians do not understand the simplicity of the gospel. We esteem wisdom higher and don't allow the Holy Spirit to rule over the church. God is going to show us some hard things and make us drink the wine of astonishment as we position ourselves in Christ. Many people not only disregard the Holy Spirit, but do not understand the operation of the Holy Spirit. If the Holy Spirit is not Lord of our life, then we cannot function or behave properly. Most Christians only have basic knowledge, and that is why the righteous scarcely make it.

Disruption is very unsettling. There is nothing complex or difficult about these topics. We are on the surface, but let us go under the water beneath the waves, to essential issues which have the effect of confusing people about what the church is actually teaching, and one is *purgatory*. We have searched high and low and can't find anyone who knows where purgatory is. The foundations of the world were discovered without one breath of purgatory. They that seek after life do not imagine things like purgatory. This will disrupt the thinking of many that truth may continue.

This is an evil against God, who laid the foundation of the earth. Go up by the mountains, and cover the earth down by the valley, and run among the hills. God has not hidden purgatory, nor has it been concealed. Those that seek after salvation rejoice and are glad; those pausing in purgatory, hell beneath is moved to meet them. Consider all of the tears because of this; they have no comforter. Purgatory is not the comforter. God looked down from heaven to see if there were any that did understand. When death seize upon us, we either pass through death or go quickly into hell. There is no remembrance of this, nor is there anything whereof it may be said see this.

Natural religion needs to be corrected, purified, and filled out by supernatural revelation. The Roman Catholic Church within the Vatican and the pope still have authority over the *entire* church, just as Peter, James, and John did, but most Christians ignore their authority.

There is no one who feels responsible for the oversight of everything that happens in the church. God shows no partiality, but in every church, anyone who fears Him and does what is right is acceptable. Not only having a correct grasp of the central points of the gospel message, but are able to walk in it This is that road that very few find.

It is reported that visual images worthy of reverence are encouraged by the church and that visual images help us to realize that God is present. They are supposed to help us to adore God. This is wrong, because this is idolatry! God is a spirit. The invisible God is clearly seen, being understood by the things that He has made. There is no such thing as a material representation of God ever. God will not overlook this as the time of ignorance. It is prayer that helps us realize that God is present. We have been persuaded to worship God contrary to the law. The mysteries of God that has been revealed must be accepted by faith. No image is worthy of reverence no matter how old it is to support our worship with God.

This disruption is like an eruption of a volcano, our distorted understanding through the generations of unsound doctrine, and misunderstood teachings brings disruption. Many churches do nothing but pass down what was given to them never discerning or searching out the matter, and with the skin of our teeth, many will barely get to heaven.

Salvation is not what we have known, but what we have done or what we have neglected to do. Christianity is that disruption that stirs up life and keeps us uncomfortable seeking guidance. Ask God who will confirm all this wisdom in truth. God sees the tares sown in among the wheat and realize the enemy has done this. He has allowed us to grow together, but now is the time to separate the wheat from the tares, and bind up the tares in bundles to be burned.

This is that disruption that suddenly takes the world by surprise, while it sits in peace and prosperity. Disruption so destructive that it is filled with the fire of the altar, that has been cast into the earth. Disruption that makes the world think about what we were taught. A last warning so disturbing that the heat of the flame shut up in the pages of the Bible is now being released.

Chapter 2

DEFINING THE LAW

Two stone tables and ten commands. Jesus summarized the ten into two. Love the Lord God with all of our heart, all our mind, all our soul and strength. And love thy neighbor as thyself. Jesus told us to keep them, do them, and teach them. It is Christ that is reconciling us to God. Jesus tells us what is necessary for perfection.

There is a righteousness of God without the law, and there is a righteousness of God with the law. An advanced transition from one to the other, like faith to faith and strength to strength. Without the law, righteousness is manifested by faith in Jesus Christ, but the righteousness of God with the law is manifested by obedience in response to that faith. We are justified by faith without the deeds of the law, but we must not forsake the established law. There must be a change in our moral behavior. This is the righteousness of God with the law. Our thinking in obeying the Word of God is that in believing the law of faith, we are justified by faith without the deeds of the law.

Teaching handed down to us teaches us that this is all that is required and we are not obligated to do the law, but that is not the case. An established law must be an obeyed law. While we are waiting for God to draw us out of sin, or away from sin, or just stop us from doing sin, yet we find that sin follows us closer. Being absolutely positive by grace we are saved through faith without the deeds of the law, and yet we fail.

We are flesh, and the sin is in our bodies. Like the sow, we wallow in the mud of the world. The lust is in our members. We must daily mortify our moral character by obeying the law. It is our duty to understand that change starts from within with the spirit of life in Christ. If we expect a change in our life through faith, then there must be obedience. Do not separate the kingdom of God from the law of God because we see the work of Christ The law has been fulfilled by the sacrifice that Jesus has made. Every sin required a sacrifice. Now every sacrifice required for our sin has been permanently provided for by the sacrifice of Christ Himself. For Christ now appears in the presence of God for us, as we present our bodies a living sacrifice to God through Christ. God has reconciled us to Himself.

Believe God for that righteousness, but after that righteousness is obtained, what's next? We are taught, and we have come to believe that we are working for righteousness if we obey the law, infact; Jesus fulfilled the law so we don't have to do anything. All we really have to do is believe in Him that justifies us, and our faith is counted for righteousness, but what's next? God can justify us, but if our moral character does not change, what is the purpose? It must be an inner desire to change our outer actions and moral behavior. Christ that abides in us will assist our decisions to change, empower us to overcome the sin of the body, and give us victory over the law of sin in the mind.

God can put righteousness in us without works, but it is our duty to maintain good works. Our nature is sinful and the heart is deceitful, so it is impossible to live in a state of righteousness without doing anything to maintain it. Pay attention to Abraham. His faith was reckoned to him for righteousness when he was uncircumcised. We walk in the steps of that faith; Abraham believed the promise, but the work began when he was circumcised. So after that we received the promise of the righteousness of God without the law, we step into the work and the righteousness of God with the law. The righteousness of faith only takes us to the next level, then the spiritual warfare begins.

Understand the work Abraham had to do. First was to show that he believed God and then show that he has obeyed God. And if that wasn't enough, Abraham, being justified by works, after having received the promise, had to offer Isaac, his son, upon the altar to perfect his faith with his works. Our work must continue in the law. The law is not dead contrary to what some may think, for the law is written in our heart.

We are free from the shackles of sin, but being free from sin could never keep us from doing what the law demands. We must be obedient. We are not bound by Old Testament civil laws. We are not bound by ceremonial laws but moral laws. We are not only shackled, but enslaved to them because they are forever inscribed in our heart. The problem is that we think that Jesus gives us this all-surpassing righteousness, but He gives us power to access the Father, something that we did not have. Jesus has reconciled us to God.

The death of Christ reconciles us to God. This is the promise. Shall we continue in sin? No, but we do because we think Christ did it all, and subconsciously we think that we have nothing to do.

Christ fulfilled the law for us, and this is what we are taught all over the world. This is the defeat not only of the Christian, but of the whole church. How shall we be able to stand before a severe judge from whom nothing is hidden, who takes no bribes nor receives excuses? The gospel is first to be reconciled with God through Christ, and then the work—to live by faith in Christ and then do His will. A life not of idleness but of labors, not of rest but to bring forth much fruit in patience.

It is clear that we must respect the law, for it is written. The Old Testament finds its fulfillment in the gospel, and without the law the gospel is incomplete. Incompleteness leaves ignorance. The law stands. We all can come to God for forgiveness of sin. Nevertheless, we take the good news of Christ's work to the world and forget the lawgiver and the law. The blood was poured out so we can approach the living God who required the blood. We go through that blood to get to God. But we need the law to function as a Christian properly. The nature of God guides our decisions in every detail of our conduct that He may be Lord and ruler of our actions.

People always talk about how sin and disobedience cannot be fixed by changing behavior, but changing behavior is exactly what changes sin and disobedience. Once we realize that we have the authority to make our own decisions, then the choice is ours to do good or evil. We have broken God's law. We have transgressed His precepts and have not done His will. If not in deed, in word. If not in word, in thought. Ignorance is a crime against God. The law must be kept; it is our duty. The debt has been paid. Let free forgiveness through Christ be faithfully proclaimed, but from the most righteous to the vilest sinner, we must put our moral behavior in line. The laws, statutes, precepts, and commandments of God are not nullified. We are hallowed and sanctified through Christ. The Father sees us joined to Christ, and our behavior must follow.

It is important to understand that our behavior must be perfect. After the matter of our pardon, when we think there is nothing left for us to do, because Jesus does it all and all we have to do is only hold out an empty hand and receive, then the spiritual battle for the soul begins to keep us from mortifying the deeds of the body. It is our actions that change the direction our life is going; for the soul that sins it shall die.

Moses, in anger, lifted up his hand, and with his rod he smote the rock twice when God said speak to the rock. Moses wrote a bill of divorcement thus changing the commandments of God, and Moses did not enter the Promised Land. This is not to slander Paul or Moses, but the Word was written for our learning. Moses was faithful; however, even Moses who spoke face-to-face with God, Satan fought with the archangel about the body of Moses because of his moral behavior. Satan has more accusations to dispute against us and our sinful thoughts and actions than that of Moses who was faithful above all the men in the house of God.

Walking after the spirit is the key to condemning sin in the flesh, but walking after the spirit should never cause us to forsake the law. We are free from sin as long as we do not obey sin or yield to sin. Crucified with Christ, a death has occurred, but not so literal as to excuse the bodily functions. It is through the spirit that we subdue by self-denial the deeds of the body. This is what changes our moral character and behavior. We would like to think that we are loosed from the law, but we are free from the restrictions that bind us being bound to the law that would cause us to obey it in our own capacity.

If the law was broken, there was no forgiveness. We were held by the consequences of breaking the law without any sacrifice or mediator to reconcile us to God. Jesus reconciled us to God enabling Him to forgive us and not condemn us when we sin against the law. The punishment was destroyed—this is what it means to be delivered from the law—and death has no more dominion. God changes not, and His law is from everlasting. It cannot be uprooted or discarded as we would like to think. Therefore, we cannot just sit in faith without doing the work of the law, and that work is done in the spirit through Christ.

Faith must be followed by the works of the law. This is a division and much controversy between two teachings; one to do away with the law, and the other to obey the law. What matters is not what Moses says, but what Christ says. The apostles seem to maintain that the law is still in force, and they must never consider a compromise to set aside the law when Jesus clearly commands the apostles to keep the law.

If we do not keep the law, then we follow after the doings of the land and walk in the ordinances of the world. The law is not necessary for salvation, neither is it necessary to obey the law in order to be saved, but we must keep the law for other reasons. If there is any truth in the Scriptures, it is in the law.

Thou shall put no other god before the only wise God. Do not make any graven images or any material representations that would help us to adore God. Do not take the name of the Lord God in vain. We must remember the Sabbath Day and keep it holy. This is a commandment. The Lord blessed the Sabbath, and He hallowed it. Honor thy father and mother. Do not forsake them when they are old. Thou shall not kill. Murder can be committed in thought and word, equally done in deed. Thou shall not commit adultery. We easily accept the fact that Moses let us write a bill of divorcement and let a woman go and be another's man's wife.

Christianity has become like the world, compromising and accepting sin. Christianity must never adapt its teaching to modem life and changing times. Life must adapt to the law. Abortion (thou shall not kill). Divorced and remarried (do not take a woman for a wife put away from her husband). Same-sex marriages (men with men and women with women); this is confusion and every evil's work. The last time the imaginations of the thoughts in the heart of people was only evil continually, God destroyed the earth. Thou shall not steal. Thou shall not covet thy neighbor's house. Do not deal falsely, neither lie one to another. Do not defraud thy neighbor. But we have cursed our neighbor and put a stumbling block before the blind by even insisting that we are not to keep the law.

This covenant God has put in our inward parts and wrote it in our hearts, our minds, and our thoughts. A covenant sealed with the precious blood of Jesus which can never be reversed. The fire shall ever be burning upon the altar; it shall never go out. These are the laws of God that we pick and choose from and decide if we are going to obey them or not. There is no good reason why we should despise the law.

Today we have made everything gods and have put them before the one who made the world. Offer unto God thanksgiving, yet prestige, power, money, and pleasures are not even a fraction of the gods that we have put before the true and living God. We worship many things. Idolatry has a deceptive form which has taken shape as an idol within us. The worship is invisible and diabolical. Rulers of darkness are targeting what is good for self (the lust of the flesh), and pleasant to the eyes (the lust of the eyes), and the things to be desired to make one wise (the pride of life). And we set up our idols, and we worship them putting them before God. We claim many other gods that demand our attention besides the invisible God.

Thus we have given an occasion to the devil to blaspheme God's holy name by our unholy actions—actions that are very subtle. Weapons of war used against us in this spiritual fight to take the name of the Lord God in vain. Our actions that sometimes go unnoticed cause us to profane God's name. Even if we don't profane His name in word, we profane it in deed. God's name is *power*, and He doesn't overlook blasphemy. Living in contradiction to His will is taking God's name in vain.

We try and make God's plan of salvation conform to our idea of what we think God means. He that says I know God and keeps not His commandments is a liar. Because there is a lack of knowledge of God, we are all guilty of ignorance and we sin because of things committed without knowledge.

Most people do not realize that the Sabbath day rest is a commandment. We think that God only said remember the Sabbath, and that is exactly what we do. The attack on the Sabbath is increasingly deceptive, drawing us into sin with many excuses for our behavior. We lightly esteem the Sabbath rest and do not take it serious. Activities dominate, and work replaces God. This shows a lack in trust in God to provide. Our demand forces others to work causing people to sin. We are people that don't trust God, and we trust in self, disregarding the Sabbath trampling the holy day of God under our feet.

We have turned the Sabbath rest into a principle. We are not freed from the technicalities of the Sabbath law, because we spiritually rest in Christ. This is the result of an evil heart of unbelief. There remains a rest to the people of God, but the Sabbath day rest is not it. Let us labor to enter into that rest. The Lord of the Sabbath will have mercy, but keep the Sabbath. We dilute this commandment. "Thou shall not work neither make anyone else work." How did we ever interpret this as resting in Christ? There is a place to enter into His rest, but the Sabbath rest is a day to rest from our week of labor.

"Honor thy father and mother." As the youth die before their parents, many days of the children are not prolonged. Our heart is wicked from our youth. A disobedient heart is painfully bad as disobeying in deed. God does not just want our actions to be right, but our hearts to be right as well. Nevertheless, our greatest parent that commands our honor and obedience is our Heavenly Father who will not only prolong our days and satisfy us with long life but give us eternal life. This is the promise being left us of entering into His rest.

Love is an action; we show love no matter how others may treat us. Everyone who hates is a murderer. Thou shall not kill, infact; whosoever is angry with his brother is as a murderer We must address the thoughts and motives behind our actions. Murder is sin. Murder begins with anger and turns to hate in the heart. Murder is not only unlawfully killing a person, but the root of murder is anger that is the motive behind the action. Even words can kill, so we must take into account how our words affect others. We are held accountable for our words. Whosoever hates his brother is a murderer. But a change in action does not lead to a work-based salvation. This is the will of God.

Lusting after a woman, thou has committed adultery with her already in your heart; thou shall not commit adultery. Many times we look at the outward actions and interpret the law with outward expressions, but God looks at the heart where man cannot see. We need to change our behavior, but first we need to change our heart. Adultery will cost us our life. Our actions have severe consequences, so even if we do not outwardly commit the sin of adultery, if we inwardly lust, we are guilty of the sin adultery. A lustful heart is an adulterous heart.

Let him that stole, steal no more. Thou shall not steal. True repentance is seen when the heart stops stealing and starts giving. Tempted and drawn away with lust and enticed. The flesh is still part of who we are. The sinful desire within the mind leads to covet. The result is taking without permission something that does not belong to us, stealing. God is trusting us to be good stewards to refuse the urge to cheat. It is a change of heart that leads to a change of direction.

To deceive is to keep from the knowledge of the truth. Satan does everything in his power to keep us from the truth. He is the father of lies. We must tell the truth. Lying lips and a deceitful tongue are an abomination unto God. Since we desire the truth, the truth may hurt throughout these pages, yet we are speaking truth in love. It is our responsibility to be honest.

The opposite of do not covet is learn to be content in whatever situation you find yourself in, whether in need or in abundance. Having a little or a lot. All commandments are sin that is committed in the mind and heart, so we must be aware of what is going on in our heart. Beware of covetousness, for a man's life does not consist in the abundance of things which he possesses. God said to keep the commandments and not just keep them but do them, for this is your wisdom and your understanding. But the nations mock the Christian because we do not adhere to all these statues. Christianity has become like the world, compromising and accepting sin. There seems to be no separation, no difference in the Christian than the world.

The law is the fire that shall ever be burning upon the altar that shall never go out. These are God's ways that we ignore. We take God lightly, and this is not a game. This is what God requires of us. Jesus's work is finished; He has reconciled us to God.

Chapter 3

THE CALL

Earth was never part of heaven, but a part of heaven was put on earth. This is not just another book of how-to or the results you will get. *This is a sound*, a declaration, and God's Word doesn't need a rebuttal. The public needs to know what kind of crisis the church is facing. It is not a matter of being argumentative, but of bringing the truth to light. Satan, the imposter of the universe, wants to trick our minds, darken our hearts, and try to persuade us to adore him rather than God. Satan is appealing to our senses and directs the power of darkness to every delectable invention from the atmosphere to the earth's surface as a deadly distraction for our eternal destruction. Satan's powers are felt more when the sinfulness of society is more evident.

Everything that God does follows a harmonious design. Just like a tree planted by a river, its fruit are these pages, as we walk through a maze. The rich juicy fruit of truth that is beneath the surface of the eternal dynamics calls from the root. Like sheep sitting in darkness, each church is on its own course striving toward the same goal.

Visions and Dreams

Understand that imagination is not faith. Imagination projects unreal images out of the mind and seeks to attach reality to them. God and the spiritual world are real. Spiritual things are here whether we see them or not. Our trouble is that we have established bad thought habits. We think of the visible world as real and doubt the reality of the invisible spiritual world. We doubt that it is real because we can't see it. The visible intrudes upon our attention and becomes the enemy of the invisible. At the root of a Christian's life lies belief in the invisible. Faith is unseen reality, and incorrect thinking is influenced by blindness. We must break the evil habit of ignoring the spiritual. For the great unseen reality is God; for he that comes to God must believe that He is.

The kingdom of God parallels our physical world, and the doors between the two worlds are open. This is not by any trick of the imagination, but a downright actuality. Here is that meditative thinking, take a bite.

Theologians, intellectual thinkers, scholars, professors, doctors, teachers, priests, pastors, and pews, there is only one in this field of expertise, and that is Christ. This is powerful, and it is dangerous, only to those who don't believe its power. This fruit comes with a great deal of meditation and reflection. Precept upon precept and line upon line, sound wisdom for the advancement of God's glory in the world.

Another book was opened for the inhabitants of the earth whose names have not been written in the Book of Life from the foundation of the world. This is a reality of the supernatural unseen world, the invisible, since what is unseen is eternal. Death and dying, seeing the dead but not seeing the spirit associated with the body, should prompt us to look well into where the dead has gone.

A child is without the thought process of a mature adult, innocent in its thinking. For to know is to reason with the power of the mind. A child is without any judgment and unknowingly accepts its reality decisively, for such is the kingdom of heaven. Adam had a childlike faith, very simple, and the consequences of sin has altered the ability to reason properly. Our thought process blocks the truth that facilitates our choices.

To measure the depth of the deep and cannot disclose where the gates of hell stand. To calculate the distance from the sun and look into the vastness of the universe but cannot detect any sign of heaven. To measure the distance of time but cannot step out of time and space alive. To step out of time and defy the natural laws that govern us. To be carried away with the clouds and float in midair. To walk across water without sinking and heal the human body with spoken word; it is no mystery why systematic knowledge considers the Bible in part myth.

We have in our mind to know good and evil. There is a threshold between right and wrong, but freedom of choice blocks belief. We must use the power to choose to see the world as it is and not the things that are seen, but the things that are unseen. We are determined to see only what we know, and we only know what we see. We doubt what we don't know or don't see and redefine laws that we don't understand.

God created man as if undecided, for we know that it repented the Lord God that He had made man on the earth. The spirit of God was hovering over the earth. God had expelled the guardian cherub and drove him from the mount of God. War broke out in heaven.

God threw Satan to the earth, and he lost his place in heaven. One-third of the angels fell with him which kept not their first estate.

These are things that have a real existence, those angels that sinned, reserved in everlasting chains, chains of darkness. God did not spare them, not exactly stripped of power, but having fallen headlong into the deep. Jesus, having been an eyewitness, saw this from the foundation of the world. He reflects on this reality as the disciples rejoice over the devils being subject to the authority they had been given. Jesus said, "I beheld Satan as lightning fall from heaven."

Now in the beginning—definitely not the beginning of God, for God has no beginning or ending—He is the alpha and omega, the almighty sovereign God. Certainly not the beginning of the ancient serpent Lucifer, beautiful and beloved, the light bearer who now dwells in darkness. It is the beginning of wickedness because wickedness was found in Satan. What punishment would be suitable for one which had a seal of perfection, full of wisdom and perfect beauty? Jealousy was the punishment since he wanted to exalt himself above the stars, above heaven, and even above the very throne of God. The thing that Satan desired the most was to rule. Then God said, "Let us make man in our image and in our likeness."

The battle was from the very origins of the world when God made us in His image. The struggle against the powers of darkness pervades the whole history of man. In the middle of His ministry, Jesus reflects on the event that happened before man was brought into existence. John, on the isles, was mirrored past, present, and future events. God hovered over the face of the deep. His spirit moved upon the face of the waters. John saw the beast rise up out of the deep wounded to death, for there was war in heaven.

Therefore, we must not ignore the destructive actions of Satan. If we ignore Satan, we will never understand the magnitude of redemption. Satan had already fallen from the foundation of the world. Here is why we see Satan in the garden in the first place. This is no coincidence. God began to create the world from the deep void, made lights and land, gathered the waters, made grass and trees, animals, birds and the bees. But God made man to rule over the devil and His angels.

Reflecting on the words of the seventy that the devils are subject unto them through his name, this is the way it should have always been, for we always had rule over them. This should not amaze us, for it was always this way. The devils were always subject unto us. In the beginning we ruled over Satan and the evil spirits. In His mercy, God sent His Son to restore us. The truth of salvation is that Jesus came to destroy the works of the devil. Satan succeeded in making us into his followers by sowing a seed of wickedness in opposition to God.

The devil opposes God, is envious of God, and is envious of man because we are made in the image and likeness of God. Satan entered the garden, his heart was corrupted with the intent to ruin us. Wickedness was present and a threat to everything God had made that was good.

There was a conflict in the divine realm. The struggle between God and Satan for the individual human soul started when Satan refused to submit to God's judgment for man to rule over him. The evil and wickedness Satan used to get control over the kingdom of this world was ingenious. Man was superior to Satan, and he was furious. Satan became a murderer from that point on being the foundation of the world, when he killed Adam with his lies. Man defied God and denounced his throne with disobedience.

Powerless to free ourselves from our own choices, we became slaves of the devil. We have distorted the divine image and likeness that we possess. Satan held us in his power until we were redeemed. God could have left us in Satan's hands forever, but in His mercy, He sent His Son to save us. Sin had deprived us of all freedom, and God offered to ransom our freedom. Nobody else, only God, could pay the price.

This is the cosmic battle. The Garden of Eden was the battleground. Adam falls through disobedience, and he loses authority to rule. Adam has eaten from the tree of knowledge to know good and evil. Up until the day wickedness was found in Satan, there was no reason why Satan could not freely eat from the tree of knowledge and the tree of life before man. This is one reason Satan lives in his wicked state. God was not going to afford man the same privilege.

These are the forces of good and evil that we approach and its mystery in the Bible. Take the book off the shelf. The choice between right and wrong is the offspring of the knowledge of good and evil. Evil in itself is not wrong until a person choses to do what evil is. To know good and evil is quite different from having to choose from good and evil. Evil worshipped what is good, and everything that God made is good. Evil had no reason to be what it is by nature. God was at peace on every side until wickedness was found in Satan.

The deep secrets of Satan knew what spirits' disobedience would release and what spirits had no other course of action but to revolt. War broke out, stars began to fall, spirits were released, and all hell broke loose. The atmosphere was in cosmic chaos, warring with the spirits of God.

Satan became the ruler of this world. The eyes of Adam and Eve were opened; they see the chaos. Today our eyes are closed blinded, lest we see with our eyes and believe with our heart. Shake off the wine and repent as this modern-day art moves in the picture frame of the mind. Adam saw with his eyes, yet he saw something radically different, something evil and wrong. Not only naked and ashamed, but naked and defenseless afraid of Satan, and ashamed of his actions. Hiding like a coward, scared he has failed God miserably.

There is not one person on earth worse than the first man, Adam, and God forgave him; therefore, the Lamb of God was slain from the foundation of the world. The mystery of God is how we witness events that was, and is, and is to come. We must not put Satan on a pedestal, but he understands what we are ever learning. These are the deep secrets of God.

The indefensible man thinks that there is no God. Evil considers this a powerful success. From the foundation of the world Satan has been intercepting arrows designed for us to conquer, arrows for our survival, for we are more than conquerors. But we are not in the right place to receive them. We think we can defend ourselves. Our position is under fire. The evil one is trying to conquer the saints. We retreat and believe the lie that we cannot rely on anything other than ourselves in our defense. But God is not weak, the battle is already won, and we have the victory.

At the very outset, death was released and hell followed. The pale horse was a direct result of the activity of Satan preparing to mount attacks against the sovereign God. The Lamb was slain, some seals were broken, and there was chaos and commotion. Evil spirits were being released into the atmosphere. The disobedience and rebellious act has caused war. Jesus spoke about the kingdom of heaven suffering violence. Since John the Baptist, the war had been intensifying with extreme force. Violence was taking it by force, and Satan knew that through death, Jesus might destroy him, and Jesus did because Satan held the power of death from the beginning.

The history that has unfolded is a glimpse of the unseen eternal. If we understand this truth, then we will begin to see evidence of things not seen being clearly understood by the things that have taken place in this life. God always does His greatest work through man's weakness and simplicity.

In the atmosphere lies powers, rulers of darkness, and spiritual wickedness. We have been blinded by a tantalizing society of modern technology, and the less this becomes believable the more it becomes a myth; where man makes rules that govern our thoughts. But this is far more real than some superstitious myth growing inside the church. God doesn't need anyone to defend Him, but we must stand at God's defense. And having done all to stand with the armor of God on, we must not take it off even for a moment.

It is important to see the things that have taken place when Adam first sinned. This is the mystery of the gospel, the answer to the seven thunders. The white horse was sent to conquer; it is the captain of the Lord of host who stands with the sword drawn. The red horse takes peace from the earth and the heart of men. The pale horse is evidence of the things not seen; when Cain killed Abel. This shows that death was present even from the foundation of the fall, Jesus was slain, and the atonement was made.

This is a mystery how John sees the hereafter, yet it is the past. Ignorance blocks our sight. From the beginning the course was set. Immediately the death sentence went into effect. It is easy to say that this is the seventh day dawning, and God is ready to rest.

It is important to see the unpleasant character and so-called genocide God condones. The God of the Old Testament is the God of the New Testament, and we raise our fist and turn our heads from the one who has created us as if He is unjust. As the workers in the vineyard complain, but as the potter He can do what He wishes with His own things, He made them. This is His world; it is His breath. Why then are we angry? There are no contradictions between the God in the Old Testament and the God in the New Testament. People just do not know God and don't understand holiness.

The act had already been completed as the veil was torn from top to bottom. This is our glimpse into the real mystery of the gospel. If you think that God is most unpleasant, imagine those in hell who love God too late, who cannot bring their life back up from the grave. This is the effect of poor choices. God created life, but look how we behave with the life that He gave us. We won't even honor God with His own breath.

Everything about grace started after the fall. There was no need for amazing grace at first. It was amazing love. So say we left our first love, and after the fall, we needed grace. God is speaking who has singled us out and extended an olive branch to us for miraculously escaping His judgment for the moment. Knowing the judgment set before us, God intervenes to help, to speak, to demonstrate, and to work among us. God is very personal. He knows that there are some things we do not know. Our wisdom is incomplete, so wisdom calls, and few be there that hear it God cannot identify with sin as we do. Satan being found with wickedness was cast out of the presence of God. Satan could do no more with his wickedness until it was sown into man. Disobedience disrupts the whole course of human existence. Evil is what evolves. The cycle by natural process recreates and gets worse and worst. The deep secrets of Satan exposed the sealed book that never needed to be opened. This was Satan's clever work for those that serve him.

God, who has been portrayed as a sinister evil God, is so loving and concerned about our sin epidemic, that He came down Himself to see us in our sins, to be touched with the feelings of our infirmities, and at all points was tempted as we are yet without sin. God then sprinkled the book and all the people with His blood.

Since the foundation of the world these things came to be, but once in the end the mystery has appeared so we all can see. We must be grateful for what God gives us, or we will never receive more than we already have. These are the invisible things clearly seen that we have witnessed with the passing of time.

God does not hide indeed; God is alive and a very present help. God is king, and we are safe in this hostile cosmic universe, a world where forces rage and chaos threatens our very existence. We struggle against evil because of disobedience. Satan works to keep us from returning to God and keeps us deceptive to his foothold. If we ever want to be active in the spiritual realm, our eyes must be open and our ears attentive to the sound.

Everything that appears is not what it seems according to Jesus. For Elijah had already come, and the disciples did not recognize him. We cannot see God, for the existence of God cannot be demonstrated scientifically. What makes us think that we can truly see the day-to-day operations and activities in the heavenly realm with our natural eyes. Everything pertaining to God must be viewed through spiritual eyes. The existence of God and immortality of the soul must be accepted by faith. Faith must prevail, it can never appeal to reason.

If a manifestation appeared through revelation, it must be met with faith. We must be walking in a place with God where we can receive it. God allows people to see visions and dream dreams, even approach His throne, yet many cannot see that the whole earth sits under a cloak of darkness. We pray that the earth aligns itself with the things that are being done in heaven; now open your eyes to see this alignment.

This is a last-day invite, come. If God with this fruit opens our eyes, the unseen world will spill over into our everyday living. Beware of them who think they have this down to the letter. If God opens your eyes, you would shake. God's presence would terrify us. To see the 01' dragon lurking, fear would grip us on every side. If God let us see the eternal warfare waging for our very lives, we all would hide. God is at war from generation to generation.

When Jesus was at the table He took bread, gave thanks, and broke it, then their eyes were opened, and they recognized him, and He disappeared from their sight. These people walked several miles with Jesus, entered into their house, did the customary washing of feet, and sat down to eat. They were looking at Jesus all the while, yet they did not see Him. They were blind, like most of us today. This is how God wants to open our eyes and impart truth that makes the stomach believe, as God searches the innermost parts of the belly.

Why is prayer so obsolete? It was prayer that opened their eyes, and it takes that same prayer to open ours. What do we expect to see when we refuse to pray and refuse to repent? As worship becomes corrupt, God is keeping up with our times. He is powerful, and His voice is echoing like a trumpet sounding at the doorway on the threshold calling, uttering things hidden since the creation of the world, saying, "Come."

We can see the atrocities of genocide in our times. Nothing happens without God. This is the problem of offending the Almighty sovereign God, for when sin has reached its full measure, we find catastrophes; like which befell the children of Israel, the holocaust, and the massacre of millions. We are living in the moment as history is being recorded, creating a Bible for the future, as we read the Bible of the past.

The corruption of biblical text could never blur the wondrous revelation of divine love. Although we have been robbed of vast riches. The Bible is a harmonious whole making it a living organism. The Bible is the Word of Him who created all things, and the authors penned their words with agreement and harmony. We should not dispute the divine origin of the Bible; it is the legacy of how it was handed down that is being exposed.

We all know now that the Romans are the root of all apostolic teaching, and that is not to say that there were not tares sown in with the wheat. If Satan had his way, we would not have a Bible today. There is no longer any reason to hide the history of the Bible or its conformity. The Bible did not arrive on a bed of roses, without conflict. We must not sugarcoat history to appease people and make the Bible have a perfect history for people to believe. If people want to disbelieve, it is their choice. God is beyond proof. God is tired of trying to make us believe. The Bible tells the stories; it gives the examples to whom have the arm of the Lord been revealed.

People of ordinary common sense want the truth, and we have a message from high heaven to deliver to them. We have been left for centuries to wander in the desert of a defeated Christian life, because of a simple presentation of the facts of the gospel that was not properly delivered. We must not be afraid to tell people what may hurt, trying to defend the gospel. We must not compromise the work of God to protect the feelings of people, as if our eternal destiny is not at stake. But with the finger of love that will go any length and stop at nothing to shock us into moral sanity.

Here is a warning: The Word of God was precious in those days, but God will not use the weight of His power to make us believe and make us obey or force us to be good. Our day and age is so cultured that it does not believe in hell, and we must not frighten people into heaven. Demon forces are great governing this world. Carnality and selfishness make our spiritual weapons as toys in the face of the enemy who takes this serious. We give ground to the monsters of hell and invite them in. These are powers of darkness, and they come in like a flood. But those who wield weapons which are not carnal but mighty through God who sees through Satan's tactics are the ones who must cross swords with this prince of darkness.

These are biblical issues and standards that we approach. The fundamental response is destructive to religion and worldviews. Leaders who have gained control and written history are the center of powers for the church; those who make decisions for the church and hold sway are being challenged by the authority of God. People maintain control by a shifting gospel. The legends and myths, doctrines of men that have been passed down, the world has become twisted, and life has become disturbed.

The overhauling of our thinking is what allows God to affect a transformation. Most of us are conformed to this world because we do not sit down and think. We go about our lives oblivious to the forces that lead and influence us. Death is so serious, that even the shadow made Jesus sweat blood. A person has missed the whole meaning of life if he has not entered into an active relationship with God through Christ.

Our understanding of God is erroneous. God's time frame is not the same as ours. The silence does not mean that, He does not see. He is waiting for us to repent and escape the damnation of hell. As someone once said, "Intoxicated with unbroken success, self-sufficient, too proud to pray to God that made us, and in the deceitfulness of our heart, we vainly imagine that all these blessings were produced by some superior wisdom and virtue of our own."

The Christian faith does not hinge upon a system of doctrines. If as Christians we fail to grasp the laws of spiritual conflict, then we will never know victory. God will not violate the freedom of man; we must be left free, or it frustrates the purpose of man's creation. It is the love of our own lives which gives Satan the advantage over us. We must be torn loose from our insane devotion to self; self-love must be removed. The disciples loved not their own lives unto death.

God does not reward faith and good behavior with material prosperity. God is not for the genocide of any human beings. People today cannot believe impossible things. Christianity has been distorted to appear ridiculous, and it is portrayed in this way. Our ultimate goal in taking the book off the shelf is to produce change in our thinking and in our life, to accomplish our real purpose, to bring the sinner out of darkness, and to lead them to the cross of Christ, the first step in the process of divine redemption.

Chapter 4

THE CALL 2

Cosmic Blindness

Here's a word of truth: know a word from the Lord for we chew it like the cud, so regurgitate this. In the deep center of our spirit we are called. When the devil discovers that your eyes are being pried opened, he will be driven mad with a sudden fierceness. Satan will begin to shoot darts of all different sorts attacking you without warning.

Day unto day reflect on the blood that is required at our hand of those that have died. We race through life never reflecting and never looking back without any implications of the direct effect our lives have had on others. We never examine or analyze the true encounter with people that we come face-to-face with. Days are swift and people are erased from our present existence. We don't have another chance to reunite with them in this life. They go and stand before the judgment seat. Whether well done or depart it is appointed once to die, twice to be born.

Did their fate lie in your hands? Ultimately they go and give an account for the choices that they have made in this life. Yet how much of an influence were we, good or bad? Days go by, and we forget what is done from one day to another only remembering days with defining moments.

Watching this spiritual war unfold is like taking a glimpse into God's realm. The church world is full of people that God has to deal with—those that run and those that hide. Measure the significance of what we see to the things that we cannot see. The transformation that takes place is like night and day. The empty space and untold stories of a missing void that we cannot replace, to the activity in the atmosphere just beyond our sight to that door that we must go through one day. As one enters the womb, another leaves the world snatched.

For some death comes swift; some are escorted through that door, others glide through, some fly through, still others are pushed through, kicked through, thrown through, beat through, forced through. Some face this door before their time, anxious to tell of the mystery existing on the other side. However, we are left with no tales to tell of a strange land pass the veil to the gulf chasm. When the time comes, the blindness fades. What role did we play, words that were never spoke, a life that we may have ignored, hindered, or helped, passed in life now a withered flower.

Reasoning beyond the most intelligent thinkers and still knows nothing. We make bright what we see and do not consider our plight of what made history. The fate that waits by the opening tunnel; open your hands, there lies the blood of another man required not killed, for we reach people one by one. Yet we reach out to massive amounts of people to produce converts and are satisfied to see a throng of people.

We lift our hands to the message we preached, groping in the dark, placing blame for the converts that retreat. But even the angels do not bring accusations against the enemy. Leaders appointed by man, not by God. It is the churches that are producing false converts. Tampering with the instructions is the least of our worries. What is our reaction toward all of this while the wind is blowing?

It is the transformation of our cast of mind and in the grounding of our character that improvement of moral growth begins. How is it that we suppose that we can do anything apart from good actions in our lives after we have become acceptable to God? We are to make ourselves into whatever we are to become, whether good or evil. We must effect our free choice, or we cannot be held responsible for the outcome.

New converts are told that human strivings and self-efforts come to an end, because everything has been done. In fact, once we see ourselves in Christ, the work is done, yet New Christians are found slipping because the life of Christ must flow through them. We find churches flooded with people looking for eternal security with the easy investment. The influx contributes to the stirring of the heart, the warning of the spirit, and the sound of the alarm. People see the signs of the times, they flood the churches and run in from the rain. People remember the story of Noah, but they are making superficial confessions, because they have no staying power.

We know that our old man has been crucified once and forever and can never be uncrucified. We are dead, yet our bodily functions still operate, so we must put to death the deeds of the body. To reckon a person dead is to live a morbid life, one with no pleasures.

The material world does not matter, where we almost cease to exist. We trust God for everything. It restricts a person, but people do not want to hear this. Because deep down inside lurks that dark sinister power of *self.* We cannot have the benefits of Christ's death while still wanting our own way. Where is the new convert in all of this?

Failure to lead a holy life is due to this false conception of the way of deliverance. The life Christ has planted in us, its nature is not to commit sin, but the matter still rests upon our choice. We must get sick unto death of sin. We must learn to not live in our feelings and believe God. Whatever contradicts the truth of God's Word, we are to regard as the devils' lie. The old life, the old world, and the old ways all are past. We do not have to never struggle to get into Christ, but we are to stay where we have been placed, to abide in Him.

To include us in Christ, God has dealt with all the members, so in our walk with God, our attention must be fixed on Christ. Clearly to go forward, we must see the purpose and importance of focusing on Christ. But a spirit-given revelation opens a door of less understanding; without the spirit in operation, for a revelation to open a person's eyes, they need the spirit.

As we enter into what God has already done, His basic principle in leading us is not to give us something or bring us through something, but to put something in us. Even as we must tell new Christians that this is not the easy life, we must tell them about the work that we must endure. Our likes and dislikes must be disregarded, our wisdom discredited, our opinion ridiculed. Of being falsely accused and our name being cast out as evil.

After we express our assurance in Christ for the forgiveness of sins and deliverance, prepare to tell them of the suffering as Christians that we must endure—the perils and exposure to character injury, persecution, afflictions, the distress, and the attacks by the enemy. Moreover, the spiritual war we face, the battles within our thoughts, the temptations, the false doctrines we must be able to detect like spiritual landmines, the accusations and abuse, and these mountains we must climb.

Then tell the new converts about the poverty, and imprisonment, and being mocked; even made to be a public spectacle. the work of discipleship, the model we must be, the orderliness we must have, the obedience we must display, the character defects that must be burned from the fiber of our being; like gold tried in the fire. Surely we are men most miserable, but we cannot put our hand to the plough and look back.

Tell the new Christian about the fruit that we must bear so we are not cut off from the rest of the tree. The pleasures that we must forsake and the money that we are to disburse. How that we must count the cost. Then tell new converts about the joys of a successful journey and how our trials are not worthy to be compared. Others might be partying, living in the pleasures of this life while we are fighting for our life to hold fast to our salvation. We better not use our time, money, or talents as we would, because they are not ours.

The flesh must go to the cross, and the power of the cross is to tear us ruthlessly from everything that would bind us to the flesh. There is nothing more tragic than to come to the end of life and realize that we have been on the wrong path. We have only one life to live down here, and we are free to do as we please with it; however, if we seek our own pleasures, our life will never glorify God. If we give ourselves unreservedly to God, adjustments may have to be made.

Most Christians have an insufficient idea of what God is asking of them, but God is asking for our very life. Even when everything seems to go wrong, stay there and be offered to the Lord. No one can be wholly the Lord's unless he is wholly consecrated to the Lord, and no one can know whether he is wholly consecrated except by tribulation. Day by day go on giving yourself to God at what the flesh finds hard. This is the attitude that God delights in, to know Him in the fellowship of His suffering.

The Christian life is an uphill battle and always a war, without intermission, and without discharge. We must learn to abide in Christ by a simple faith. God is not going to show us everything at once. No soldier is made in a day. It is a lifelong process, a lifelong attitude. To get people in touch with God, we must present Him through Christ.

We have discovered a tradition where God deals with man through the persuasion of Christ's death. As a sinner our call is to salvation, but as saints, our call is to suffering. All the seeming beauty of life under the sun is to be stripped away, and we are left with *God alone*. We preach Christ Jesus, but our supreme task is to press upon men the claims of Christ in a wholehearted surrender and obedience.

No one is moved by love anymore. Our gospel has ceased to grip souls, because we compromise and use the language of compromise. If we are speaking the truth in love, we are first to love God. If we love God, then we shall speak the truth to others. This is a call. The knowledge of sin is obvious; it is the deception of sin that is subtle. We have effectively barricaded our hearts against God's mighty love and that our halfhearted love for Jesus is the shame of the church.

We allow the self-life to exist, and self must be dethroned. Self is not only the seat and habitation but the very life of *sin*. If that sin is not denied, that it is rooted in self. By taking up the cross daily, then we see Christians fall and spiritual leaders stumble. The law is written in our hearts and the law exposes sin, but it is the cross that destroys it.

We are not to break one commandment and not for justification purposes or to justify ourselves in any way, but for obedience. This is our labor of love. This cuts people to the heart. Grace is a defense that helps when under it. The law is at the top of most religious mistakes because we see grace and push the law aside. The harmony between the law and grace has produced error. The enemy has created havoc hiding sound doctrine. We are called to live to a higher standard by the abundant grace that God has made available through Christ Jesus.

Our failure shows our need for grace, and we must not give every occasion to the flesh because we are under grace. We are to labor to enter in. Grace is to work in us. God is worthy of the highest obedience from His creation. We step over God's law with a total disregard, trespassing the boundaries God has marked out. The Christian is to forfeit the present and choose to suffer for a season. The world, its joys and its pleasures, are for a season. Our call is to reign with Christ.

Religious leaders, with their heightened sense of self-importance, coupled with influence and a high view of *self*, the energy of the flesh spoils God's work. God does not exist for man. If Satan can make us covetous people, trying to satisfy ourselves on life, then he has ruined our ministry. The chief and highest end of man is not to glorify self. Self is the root, the branches, in fact—the very tree of all evil.

God chooses His spiritual leaders in the furnace of affliction—leaders that can never be made by man, neither by councils, nor by conferences, societies, synods; neither can schools make them, but

God only. Remember, not many wise men according to the flesh, not many mighty, not many noble are called.

We must be wise in our spiritual pursuit understanding the delicate situation concerning true knowledge of God. As we look well at the things set before us, God alone is free from error. Infallibility should be discarded because it has been disproved by historical and biblical research. No one is guaranteed immunity from error when they define doctrine. No church teaching is automatically free from error.

Pronouncements when ratified by the pope are held to be infallible. Scripture could be interpreted only by the so-called infallible pope. However, the true message of God in Christ Jesus has prevailed because of His life, death, and resurrection that has set in motion a movement which over the course of time has removed revelation and the operation of the Holy Spirit and took on an institutional form. If we cut through to the basic simplicity of the tradition handed down, stripped to the bare necessity of scriptural survival, we can see that it has been developed and expounded upon by a direct revelation from God and the Holy Spirit.

When we consider what has been written, it says that the whole world wanders after the beast. We must look at what we have been taught, what we teach, how we perceive the truth, and how much do we really know about God. Our conscience cannot be captive to the Word of God if we don't search for the truth. It is harmful for believers to have a false sense of security. If we are on the right path for the truth, few be there that find it. Love will not hide truth, and true love will guide people to safety from the horrors of deception and spiritual lies.

For God to make us eternally secure, then we must become better and not just by wishing for it. This would involve doing nothing at all. For if mere improvements were to be achieved simply by a wish, then everybody would be good. Character does not change for the better by improving the flesh, but by allowing it to be replaced by the Holy Spirit.

Abiding in Christ and Christ in us is difficult. To perceive the process by which Christ wants to abide is not simple. The proposed process of living in the spirit is elusive. Just to say, trusting in the Holy Spirit to do what we cannot do ourselves is not a definite measurable way of responding. Therefore, we look to the spirit of God to produce in us wisdom.

Every day we are learning not to take any actions without relying on God. We must find no sufficiency in ourselves. We must put no reliance on ourselves. Anything that we can do without prayer and without an utter dependency upon God comes from the flesh. We can do nothing apart from God. Christ is planted in us, and this life grows in us until the very likeness of Christ begins to reproduce in our lives. We must let God live His life in us.

Death and the resurrection must remain an abiding principle of our lives. We are by nature utterly helpless. Vast areas of our life is inconsistent with the faith we profess because it is not expressed in our character. We must rely upon the indwelling Holy Spirit. An inner battle rages that blocks out the still small voice of God. Satan conspires to surround our lives with interfering noises and distractions that drown out the voice of God. We cannot be true followers of Christ without a rule of life that leads chaos within us toward obedience to God. We are all confronted with the call to return to the Lord God; this is what is being sounded.

Nevertheless, desire swells up in us, and we face temptation daily. Deliberate sin pins us in a corner, habitual sin follows us, and unknown sin attacks us. We are under grace, yet we find that our sins are those described under the law. We obey the laws of the land or suffer the consequences. We are careful to abide by societies' rules and regulations and not offend them. If only we thought that way about God's laws. What an underlying current of unaddressed issues. It is the lack of understanding that results in habitual failure and sinning. If we don't live in the spirit, then we find habitual sin, deliberate sin, lust, and the desire to sin making our life quite a contradiction of the fact that we are in Christ.

No one is immune by the attacks of Satan, as we wait for the next shocking wave of events. This is the reality of everyday life as we walk in the world. We try to serve God and the world at the same time, and we are not distinctive. Our power in the world lies in our difference from the world. The law still stands, but our moral standards are low. Grace keeps us obedient to the law. In fact, the elements of all sin will find its origin in the law. Our faith by our works is our obedience to the law, then grace gives us the power to walk in obedience. Our righteousness must exceed the righteousness we see in society. To exceed in righteousness, we must obey outwardly and inwardly.

A revelation is from the Holy Spirit that brings to light hidden things with holy interpretations. We must intellectually sharpen and develop our mind. But the immature Christian that is not growing spiritually or producing fruit will suffer under attack whether by lack of unlearned truth, making them ignorant to the knowledge necessary for survival, or by lack of strength, for we have no power in ourselves to do what God requires.

Christian thinking looks at issues and ideas from a standpoint of what God desires and what gives Him honor. Spiritual growth is a mental growth that will cultivate Christian perspectives. We must have a Christian thought process helpful for those who are struggling, because a person can choose a life of rebellion willfully and deliberately. Selfdiscipline is our choice.

There is much misunderstanding if we regard the law as rules which can be obeyed literally by anybody under any circumstances by the exercise of the human will. We can do no good thing without divine assistance. To have the spirit within us is to have the living God within us. As earthen vessels we carry a treasure of unspeakable worth, and with the spirit of God within, there are resources enough in our heart to meet the demand of every circumstance in which we will ever find ourselves.

Many Christians do not experience the power of the Holy Spirit. Some Christians live victorious lives while others are in a state of constant defeat. Some Christians recognize the divine ownership of their lives, while others are still their own masters. Not until the Holy Spirit is given His full place can He reproduce the life of Christ in any believer. Many Christians are truly saved yet bound by sin. Unless our eyes have been opened, to see that we have died in Christ, it is unthinkable to ever experience the Holy Spirit's power. We must proclaim ourselves dead and fit only for the grave. It is to bring an end to everything in us that is not of God.

As Christians we will experience failure to keep the law. Whatever sin that is committed by anyone will find its origin in the law. We know that all have sinned, and anyone who says that they have no sin is a liar. By lying we recognize the evil. Lying is both the cause and manifestation of evil. This is what it means to come boldly to the throne of grace to get mercy, and in all thy getting, get an understanding. When temptation is at the point of sin, that grace is there to help in the time of need.

We are still hunted and haunted by the carnality of the flesh. Jesus knows that we cannot keep the law, yet the law of God stands tall like a beacon of light. We do not live under the law, but we must obey it. Jesus fulfilled the law under the old covenant by accepting its punishment; therefore, we have Jesus with a stern rebuke to obey the law and teach men to do so. Nevertheless, people have made little or no response to his moral demands.

We must examine ourselves, speak these things, and do according to the law that our conduct may stand in the will of God. Remember that it is God who accomplishes the work. God's requirements have not altered, but we are not the ones to meet them. Moreover, we are not to run around making a mockery of the law. Everything makes sense in its simplicity. We are to love God still, and we are to love our neighbors. Let us not be ignorant and try to live out Jewish traditions.

Chapter 5

WHO IS PAUL?

The guiding forces are faith and love. Self-righteousness and complacency are today's greatest sins. The trouble is that the pure Word of God has been overlaid and weighed down with false hopes. The call that goes forth must be followed by the response of obedience. Our future depends on the right understanding. Jesus teaches us to obey the law, and these things have nothing to do with the gift of salvation. However, if we want to be perfect, then we must keep the law. In fact, Jesus asks nothing of us without giving us the strength to perform it.

For the superstructure of elite, capable, and affluent leaders, the institutional and doctrinal elements in the preaching act as obstacles to Jesus and His Word. Jesus taught no theology whatsoever because His teaching is entirely spiritual. No one can see without the illumination of the Holy Spirit. The revelation of the suffering Messiah is itself the gospel, and the kingdom of God and its gospel are essentially supernatural. The church has already erected a spiritual tyranny over people by dictating what we must read and believe in order to be saved. Christians think that we are not under the law but under grace.

Grace is represented as the church's inexhaustible treasury, showers of blessings with generous hands without question, without fixed limits, without price or cost. This type of grace is a doctrine, a principle held to be sufficient enough to secure remission of sins, and in it we find that there is no real desire to be delivered from sin. Grace alone does everything, and everything can be had for nothing. But everything remains as it was before, and we are still sinners. With this free and boundless grace of God, we live like the rest of the world.

We model ourselves after the world's standards. We rebel from living a life of obedience to the commandments of God. For the world has been justified by grace. We are taught that we better not strive against this indispensable grace. We are comforted and, rest assured, in possession of this grace. This grace is deadly, yet this is the love of God, taught as the Christian idea of God. This grace calls for obedience because God paid a price for our life. It cost a man His life; this cup cost His blood.

What grace really means is to follow Christ on the path of absolute loyal obedience. To live the Christian life, we must renounce the world in order to learn obedience. Pure grace does not offer exemption from obedience to the command of Christ. God's forgiving grace does not automatically grant the world righteousness and holiness. The call must be exercised in the following of Christ. The commandments must be in harmony with perfect obedience in our daily life.

Taken from the letters of Paul, grace alone can save, but we leave out the obligation of discipleship assuming that we already know this. The sin is in the world; it is the sinner that needs to be transformed to following Christ with a radical selfrenunciation.

Grace is God's answer, but we cannot stop for one moment chasing after Him. We are taught, and it has been preached more ways than one that we live the Christian life, and then we go and sin as much as we like and rely on grace to forgive us. After all, the world is justified in principle by grace. We cling to our worldly existence and remain as we were, except with the added assurance that the grace of God will cover us. It is under this influence that the world has been made Christian. Grace has ceased to be the gift of God; what is required is obedience.

This is that wickedness and half-truth. An evil lie from the father of lies, a subtle deception, destined to cause us to spend eternity in hell. These tactics brought us death from the foundation of the world through Adam and Eve. Satan is playing for keeps. Our eternal destiny is in jeopardy. It is no mystery that our lives are on the line, and there are no second chances.

To hand people a doctrine and expect them to believe the validity without them searching for the truth and weighing all the evidence is like a treasure hid in a field, for it is the glory of God to conceal a matter, but we buy the field without even searching to see if the field contains the treasure. Christ has authority to call us and demand our obedience. The call to follow Christ is the narrow way, and Christ calls us to follow Him.

To use God's Word as a big stick on Him; to try and keep God in line with our ideas and principles, we stand on dangerous ground. We are taught and told that our salvation has already been accomplished by the grace of God. However, to sin and rely on grace, the grace which God has given us, this is extremely dangerous. There is nothing worse and more sinister than a devilish abuse of grace. This is what we preach, and this is what we teach. This is why we stumble, and new converts are being defeated.

Barred from knowledge because we have hidden it, hardened in disobedience, deceived, and weakened. Let us touch and agree, lest you think us guilty of denying substantial teaching of Scripture. Our servitude, unknowingly to the world, is our dedication to God, and God is looking for faith as He approaches. We have not only the power, but the obligation to pull the whole world to safety after us and point the way for others.

The road to faith passes through obedience. We are held before the world, promising Christianity is rich in spiritual fruit, showing many outward signs of being religious, yet we are barren, rendered unfruitful, and in fact, dying. Salvation is by faith alone, but the call vanishes into thin air if we imagine that we can follow Christ without taking the steps of obedience to keep the commandments. To close our eyes to such spiritual evidence comes dangerously near to sin against the Holy Spirit. Our teaching is not incorrect as much as it is incomplete.

This is a direction from God, which makes an absolute claim on our obedience. We should serve God with our intellect as well as our spirit. We are hopeless if we have closed our mind to the living Word of God. How serious we rage against the commandments and the obedience it demands. Jesus makes the commandments unmistakably clear.

The very thought that God has forgiven us of our sins despite our inadequacy brings comfort, but to live in fellowship with Him, we must be obedient to Him. No one is justified by doing what the law commands; we are justified as a result of our trust in Christ. Keeping the law is not the way to win acceptance with God, but the gospel of salvation by grace through faith in Christ should not remove all incentives for moral effort.

Time and distance have thrown up barriers between us and biblical writers which block our understanding. We must understand all the essential things that God wants us to understand for our eternal salvation. To be justified means to be put in right relations with God. It is important to realize that being put right with God involves a subsequent total change in our moral behavior. Jesus teaches us to keep the commandments, but the commandments are not essential for salvation. There is no path to salvation lying in that direction.

Paul was a fanatic, crucified with Christ, but Paul's gospel was really another gospel. However, Calvary was the inspiration for Paul's missionary achievements. It was the soul of his preaching. It was the foundation upon which he built the temple of his Christian life. The gospel of Paul was the cross of Christ; the cross of Christ was the power of God and the wisdom of God. We do not seek to discredit Paul's message, and we must not deny this nor be in ignorance of Paul's life. We must have a great appreciation for Paul, but who is Paul?

Christian unity is dear, but truth stands before the throne. Truth inflicts pain, and we must insist in its pain. Controversy is not the objective. The cross was the supreme goal of Christ. Paul was a thinker trained in the greatest schools of his day, one who breathed out threatenings and slaughters. The long-awaited Messiah was crucified, and Paul had missed it. Paul had a brief vision, and so we accept the New Testament literature of Paul. Paul's salvation came by faith, and if we can understand the way Paul received salvation, then we may begin to see how he thinks. Paul believed the promises of

God, but it was the grace of God that came to him, the chosen vessel. Yet Paul was still hostile to the disciples.

Christians were bold and assertive spreading what Paul considered blaspheme. Head of the great persecution, breathing threats against the disciples, the same disciples that Paul must now rely on. No one thinks to question Paul, but Jesus had twelve disciples that He taught. Who is Paul? The structure of the New Testament has Peter's gospel being replaced with Paul's gospel. But Paul could lay no claim to having been in the company of Christ; he had no first-hand knowledge of the life and ministry of Jesus. The disciples had unity because they were in the presence of God. Paul's were the earliest surviving Christian documents.

Paul was obedient to the call, and we take Paul's words but do not follow Christ with the acts of obedience. Jesus said, "If thou will enter into life, keep the commandments." Paul said, "Are ye so foolish, are ye now." But who is Paul? We must not think of obedience to the commands of Jesus to observe the law as trying to finish by natural means the process that began supernaturally.

God has always used men with nothing and little academic experience to point the way for others. Peter, the head of the Jewish Christians, unschooled and unlearned, or Paul, head of the Gentile Christians, highly educated. This conflict was before the books of the New Testament had been completed. These Christian conflicts were struggles over power and not just theology. These disciples walked with Christ; Paul came later.

The lack of intellectual love for God does not worry us. We think that we do not need our mind to serve God; there has been a mistake. We have tried to wake people up, but they seem to have sunk to the level of their surroundings. The controversy is still smoldering. We see people still being circumcised, and some are uncircumcised. Some people keep the Sabbath day on Saturday, and some people keep it on Sunday. These conflicts are still felt and affect our worship today.

Furthermore, if we understand the church history, isn't it ironic that the Roman Empire who crucified Jesus is the same Roman Catholic Church who has established Christianity throughout the world? And why do people think that Peter was in error? Peter is a disciple, and we have not let Peter become a fisher of men. The mind-set of society has changed, evil is still working. The Western culture has nothing to do with the story of Christ, but because of ignorance and a refusal to seek the truth, we evade the revealed will of God.

How does Paul's brief vision nullify the teachings of Jesus, witnessed by Peter and the disciples? We so easily accept Paul over the handpicked apostles. Paul had a strong distaste for the law. Paul underestimated the disciples' earthly knowledge of Christ. Paul's refusal to go to Jerusalem, his rising indignation toward the pillars Peter, James, and John, their peculiar position of favor, and their personal distinctions which by Paul's definition is not the way that God works. It was this type of attitude that made it possible for a thorn.

Paul was jealous, and he was defiant; the disciples added nothing to him. Paul was not willing to accept any further instructions; he was independent and wanted to prove the supernatural origin of his ministry. Our records wipe out the response of Peter, and all we are left with is Paul. "Salvation by faith through grace, it is the gift of God," the easy Christian life. Yet Paul never reflects on how obedient he was to the call. He cried, "Lord! What will thou have me to do?"

Faith is only real when there is obedience, and faith only becomes faith in the act of obedience. Paul was a thinker, highly educated, and well versed in the knowledge of the Scriptures to impart with the twelve who were unschooled and unlearned. Paul's resentment toward the apostles rose because of their distinguished, notable, and distinct rising fame. Paul was familiar with being notable; he was use to a position of authority, who was above reaching up to the apostles.

Paul was never caught up into the third heaven himself, but he knew a man caught up into paradise and heard unspeakable words while he himself was given a thorn in the flesh. However, that thorn was self. For Paul, one of the subtlest forms of self is to blame the devil. Conscious of his insecure position, Paul was hurt as people accused him of being no true apostle. For if thou will be perfect, then we cannot covet after an easy Christian life.

All law is biblically based; these principles are the absolute standards that exist in the world today by which all moral judgment of life is measured. We are taught that we are not under the law but under grace, a grace without obedience to the law. Understand Paul's thought here that a return to the commandments is impossible, yet understand Peter's position having been commanded by Jesus to keep the commandments and teach men likewise.

By God's laws, the laws of the land were created, and if that wasn't enough, they are written in our hearts. If we are not under the law, then we think that we are not obligated to abide by the law. This pattern of thinking has affected our minds to the point where we deem it unnecessary to obey the commandments. We disregard the Sabbath day and do not love God with all of our intelligence. We cannot love our neighbor until we learn to love God, and we cannot love God until we learn to keep His commandments.

We refuse to use our mind to serve God and are ignorant in our understanding. For God speaketh once yea twice, yet man perceives it not. Paul, he was chosen by Rome, but what has issued from this Centuries later is complete ignorance as the world stands in darkness. The souls of many have been sunken by imagined perils. It has turned them from the true way. Yet no one is afraid that we may forfeit heaven. We run to Paul with his high counsel; Paul above all other works, above all other disciples. God's will has been taken from the smallest circle, the twelve disciples; beautiful for situation, the one who un-wills what He wills. These are the things plucked up that chain down many, turning their course.

The strict decree is broken as we lay trust in a speech, from a vision, that honors God, and all honors it instead of God. The fallen Christians are those who have no intellect. We must realize that we are accountable to God. It is extremely important because our life depends upon the path that we take, and the path we take depends upon the knowledge we know. Revelation is from God, and there is no authority except from God. The way to truth and freedom is to accept these difficulties as from God. If these are Satan's troubles, then they must have gotten by God to get to us. We have all walked along this same warn path beaten out and paved by others. We are carving out the path that have always existed, the true tribe of Christians, to make war with those who have invested in deceiving us.

"Oh, these are parts of His ways, but how little a portion is heard of Him, but the thunder of His power who can understand." This is a sound!

After the death of the arch rivals, Peter and Paul, the conflict continued. It is distinctive, revolutionary, compelling, and dangerous. Two groups arose like Peter and Paul in the early centuries after the historical crucifixion and resurrection. The Ebionites, the Jewish Christians for Peter, and the Marcionites, anti-Jewish Gentile Christians for Paul and his distaste for the law. Here we may get a better understanding of the intensity of the conflict that ensued between Peter and Paul.

The Ebionites believed that all Jews and Gentiles must observe the commandments, that Jesus was the Jewish Messiah sent from a Jewish God to a Jewish people in fulfillment of the Jewish scriptures. They insisted on observing the Sabbath, keeping kosher, and circumcising all males. The Ebionites, however, were poor by choice, and this is the true meaning behind their name. Unschooled and unlearned, with less means to pass down tradition. The Ebionites did not accept Jesus's preexistence or virgin birth, but they also did not have our New Testament. Therefore, they understood Jesus differently.

Marcion, like Paul, was one of the most significant Christian thinkers and writers of the early centuries known as the Marcionites, where the Jewish customs are rejected and the Pauline revelations are completely distorted. As we look back at how these people portray God, their conception was how could the same God be responsible for both being the wrathful and vengeful God of the Old Testament Jews and be the loving merciful New Testament God of Jesus. But the Marcionites doctrine originates from the preaching of Paul. The Marcionites maintained that Jesus was a mere man but chosen by God at His baptism to be the savior of the world. This entire doctrine is based on sacred text, a teaching that does not worship Christ as God. This type of doctrine has resurfaced, and it is not so obvious to detect.

If Christ is God and God is God, then how can there be only one God? This is causing huge problems. It was a threat to the church then, and it is a greater threat now. We have thinkers who try to enter into another man's line of work without permission, trying to make sense of Scripture that is completely inspired. Christ is both God and man. There is only one God. Christ was the Father Himself who came in the flesh to save the world that He created. Such a holy God. How else can God identify with us? He could have never understood sin as us.

If Christ is God, then He must be that one. The doctrine of the Trinity is not the answer. Let us never try to work out a precise understanding of God. For God is not God if He is not one. It is impossible to have two beings who are supreme, because if two of them exist, then neither one of them is supreme, and for God to be God, He must be completely supreme. Our neglect of the truth allows the devil to pick away at our foundation, and God is removed from our intellectual thinking.

One by one we must answer to God. His laws are rooted in His infinite wisdom and understanding of the nature of man. Christ brought us not from under the law, but from under the curse of the law. However, Paul is reproved by James in Jerusalem about teaching the Jews which were among the Gentiles to forsake the law of Moses. Paul could not expound on the teachings of Christ, and he refused the instructions of the disciples. It is not right for Paul to teach the way that he does, and we find people like Marcion who draws their own conclusion to the gospel presentation. Paul's statement that we are trying to obtain right standing with God through obeying the law is direct defiance to what Jesus specifically told the disciples to do: to keep the commandments. We cannot teach rebellion to God and obedience to Christ.

If you think that this is an attempt to lay again heavy burdens by demanding meticulous obedience to the law itself and the elaborations of it, then you have not grasped the spiritual principle. The yoke is easy because it is not really obedience to any external law. It is first loyalty to God which enables us to do easily without feeling we are struggling under a heavy burden of what God would have us to do. We are so preoccupied with the natural, that we are unable to recognize the supernatural. We are looking for the coming of the external reign of God over the world and not His reign over our hearts.

We are still living in that long-expected great and dreadful day of the Lord where the simplicity of God's message is ruined, His redemptive work is disregarded, and greed for personal gain, false philosophies, and erroneous doctrines have produced a perverted morality. The accumulation of wealth is so absorbing that it gives its victims a false sense of values, contradictory to the character of Jesus, whose life was characterized by humility and poverty.

The Pharisees were offended, today we expect nothing less. We are still teaching, allowing, confirming, compromising, and agreeing on doctrine teaching which are the commandments of men, having made the commandments of God ineffective.

Our faith is inspired by love. Love is the fulfilment of the law. We teach that we are justified through faith, but faith follows obedience. We are selfish people, because we are comfortable with the work of Christ. Unbelief is our biggest obstacle. There lies an impenetrable barrier to belief, and God will not force belief inside of us. We have added so many complicated rules and regulations to biblical teaching that it not only obscures Bible views, but it defeats the purpose for which God has intended.

Salvation is entirely a matter of God's grace, His goodness and generosity, and not of any human merit. Conceiving the idea that good moral conduct is wholly irrelevant, we have done harm to others. We are not insisting at all on works of the law as grounds of acceptance with God. Obedience shows love toward God, and we love God by faith. Here lies a fundamental principle: to inherit eternal life, to be drawn to the kingdom of God, keep the commandments. God is to be loved with every faculty of our being, and love our neighbor as ourselves. The greatest commandment in the law makes love the dominate motive.

The world has become rotten with evil. Deception is and has always been crafty and witty as the latest highly advanced technological engineered invention, complex and more invisible in its subtle form than the air we breathe. If we failed to prepare, the day of opportunity will have passed forever and the door will be shut, and we will be permanently barred.

Chapter 6

HEAVEN OR HELL PART 1

We are in a battle to fight back the hands of hell. For hell starts on the path we take, enticing and inviting us with a wide mouth words that climb the gates and call. This is an intense revelation with a heightened understanding of religion and theology with no human intelligence existing. There is a dramatic impact to be felt in the world, a spiritual awakening, for the general populace, the church, and the academic world. An end-time revelation set forth in these pages for the last warning.

We are keenly attuned to religion and theology as a widely accepted path to righteousness, but there is a profound difference between the study of human behavior and the study of God. We must bind and abhor any deception which hides truth from our sight. The self-disclosure and supernatural revelation from the mind of God to us are human authors. Whether it is their own unaided opinions and insight instead of being endowed under the inspiration of the Holy Spirit is something God must reveal. Revelation is something that God does.

Christianity has concerned itself with theological and doctrinal questions which have no part in gospel teaching. This is a hard saying, and it is dangerous, but Jesus taught no theology whatsoever. All the doctrines and theologies of the churches are human inventions. Many people have rejected the divine inspiration of the Scripture and cry hell is in the mind, and hell is here on earth, or that hell is a state of being. But the reality is that hell follows death, and we know that death is real.

The gates of hell are likened to a two-way mirror. The inhabitants can see out, but we that are among the land of the living, who cannot see in. There is only one that brings us a report every day and can travel through both doors of reality, and his name is death; and hell follows.

How we understand the nature and character of God influences how we understand the nature of man who bears God's image. We have furbished God to a peripheral status of insignificance in the life of the church. The orchestration by some of its leaders that conform their religion to the world brings empty worship which is taking from God and giving to self, as the central focus of faith.

When the people saw that Moses delayed coming down, when the people saw that God took a long time coming, the people sat down with a false knowledge of God and rose up to play. We are elevating human traditions to the level of divine authority. Even with Paul, the letter killeth, but the spirit giveth life.

The church is called to be always reforming. It is our duty of this generation of Christians to pass on our tradition, a legacy that will insure we are consistent with apostolic tradition. The spirit unlocks the mystery of biblical teaching. Externally the Bible is a collection of inspired documents, seldom originals. The names of the actual writers are seldom known, but it does not affect the spiritual purpose of the Bible. The biblical roots and spiritual truths, the actual route by which it reached its present form does not matter. It is our destiny that is on the line.

Welcome to the Gates

Good or evil, eternal torment or eternal bliss, hell is a different concept to be understood. If the gates of hell can prevail, it can only be through false teachings; therefore, the entrance to hell starts there. The gates of hell cannot and will not prevail against the church. Individually we are the church; one by one we make up the body. Yet we find the church overcome, overrun, trampled by its doctrines and teachings. We call the church back to its apostolic and biblical roots. We are in a spiritual struggle for our eternal destiny.

We can never bind what we do not know, and we can never loose what we cannot see. In fact, infant baptism is not relevant to God's purpose and Christ's work. It has absolutely nothing to do with pleasing God. We make things more complex than God intended to the point of injury, because of our ability to reason, for there is one baptism. It is not a point of error, but it is a diabolical tactic to prolong and postpone the true work of God with centuries of debate about insignificant issues.

Christian churches have neglected to make Christian teachings clear to people. Godly intelligence is just a part of the Christian message as is love. Once we begin to raise our thoughts toward God, it makes communication possible for God to deposit in our minds the knowledge of Him. The Bible is inspired by God. Church creeds and pronouncements are the work of men.

The underlying currents are the unseen spiritual forces, rulers, and powers of darkness. As the issues grow darker, the spirit blows harder. The acceptance of truth involves the scrapping of all the old standards. God cannot wait for us to be spiritually ready for *change* to accept truth; the time is now. Jesus lays the axe to the root of these horrible traditions that have set us on a course straight for hell. If the tares are being bound in bundles, then you see that the harvest time has come. How long did we expect to grow together, for sin has reached its full measure. Our slowness and reluctance to perceive the right path will have our soul endangered for hell's fire.

Truth always works, truth always heals, and truth always turns out to be consistent when thoroughly sifted. There are false teachers of true religion who bring half-truths in sheep's clothing. Although they are perfectly sincere in their claims and pretensions, they come between the seeker and the saving truth. And despite their good intentions, they are spiritual wolves.

Our progress on the right path may be slow, but keep on the path, for it is better to process information slowly on the right path than to be standing before the gates of hell until they open because of ignorance. Here is seeing God; to see God is to apprehend truth as it really is. Blessed are they who recognize Him. Satan has gained entry into the church. We debate the Word of God with some of the most volatile controversies and escalated debates ever recorded.

The authority of the church has placed the church above the Scriptures and made the Scriptures less important than the church. When they did not like the Scriptures, they completely changed them. Who gave the church the power to judge the Scriptures with a nod of authority and a stamp of approval, making God's Word authentic? This is the legacy left for us, and we are left without any excuse as to why. The legacy we must leave comes with a greater responsibility of handling the Bible more carefully and accurately. How can we ever withstand the judgment of a holy and just God?

Take sin seriously because sin offends God. Every sin is an act of treason that insults God's glory. We take sin so lightly, but the soul that sins shall die. In this fallen world, we try to bind God to our ideas and principles. We soon forget the real terms of the life we live; God's promise of life is on the condition of obedience.

God and His holiness can never justify sin. We must harden ourselves against every sympathy for sin. We teach that we are justified through faith, but faith follows obedience. There is no justification for our actions and wrong choices. There was no justification for Adam's disobedience, because he still died. We can never justify wrong. When we sin, we are never right and we are never innocent.

It is one thing to struggle with difficulties in interpretation, but it's another thing to distort the meaning of God's Word. Satan's strategies are to use the Word of God to authorize a belief or practice that goes against the character of God. To be justified means to be put in right relations with God. Furthermore, it is important to realize that being put right with God involves a subsequent total change in our moral behavior.

Justified should take on a new meaning. The justification of the sinner, which is the grace of God, has become the justification of sin. Justification is complex, more complex than God intended. God has extended His hand to receive us into His favor as if we were righteous. In God's sight we are treated as if we are righteous with the imputation of the righteousness of Christ. However, there is still the thing of justification. For who is man that God is mindful of him enough to be obligated to reward our sins when our righteousness is as filthy rags? The heart of this controversy has just been overthrown.

Not under the law, but under grace—overthrown. There is no such thing as the Trinity uprooted. Infallibility, overthrown. Infant baptism, uprooted. Predestination, overthrown. Assurance, uprooted. Eternal security, overthrown. "I will overthrow what I have built," saith the Lord, "and uproot what I have planted throughout the earth."

We mean well in what we intend to say, but we are using the wrong terminology; with our heightened sense of academic achievements, we are using technical vocabulary to describe the only wise God, and we fail, disrupting simple salvation. We cannot describe with any words found in our vocabulary or in any language the nature, character, or work of God. His work is incomprehensible. Be prepared to travel the narrow way of personal commitment to Christ and self-renunciation, for there is no alternative entrance. What makes the narrow path hard to find is the existence of numerous false teachings.

The Roman Catholic Church is the foundation for all Christian churches. These are our roots; therefore, seeing the root, we can see why all tithes are appealing to church leaders, as well as the insincere congregation. The impression that we could purchase salvation simply by giving tithes and that alms must be given in a proper spirit to be effective in buying our way into heaven is utterly ridiculous.

The only merit that can avail for the sinner is the *blood of Jesus Christ*. Christ and His suffering, God counted it worthy for our way to heaven. We can never make sin right. God will never make sin right. That is to say justify sin. God will cover sin and wash us, atone the sin, and remove it far from us, but there is no justification for sin. Salvation does not rest in us. The church cannot redeem us. Only Christ alone can save us, which brings us to the doctrine "Once saved, always saved."

If we can never justify sin and our righteousness is as filthy rags, what could make us think that if we sin we will continue to be saved? True faith is proved by obedience; without the aid of good works, our faith is dead. Live faith produces real work. If no work follows our profession of faith, then our salvation is dead.

Justification by faith alone; once saved, always saved; the deadly enemy grace sufficient to secure the remission of sins is the justification of sin without the justification of the sinner. These are doctrines and principles, the results of the gates of hell. Welcome. God will justify the sinner, but God will never justify sin. Sin is wrong. God will never make sin right, that is to say that it is okay to do. In fact, God does not make us right; it is the blood that He has given upon the altar to make an atonement for our sins that makes us right.

The risk that the church took in the use of the term once rejected is a threat today, as the world embraces the doctrine of the Trinity. It is not that the unity of the Godhead does not exist, for there are three that bear record in heaven—the Father, the Word, and the Holy Spirit. God's Word could never be touched. It just prospered where it was sent. But when the Word of God became flesh, the invisible things became clear. It is the title man has associated with what we already know to be true in the Scriptures that is offensive to God. Man is always trying to take credit for what God has perfected concerning us. This doctrine or principle makes the church look like we worship a triad of gods, which is idolatry, making man the chief and highest end for his proclamation.

Every man has his work, and to the watchman it is to watch. The watchman watches and prays. Know that the effectual fervent prayers of the righteous avails much. As Moses was the mediator of the old covenant, Jesus is the mediator of the new covenant. A holy covenant that was sealed with His blood. Many times Moses fell upon his face pleading to God for the people as a mediator, and God relented.

Jesus, God with us, died a sinner's death on the cross, who manifested His perfect union with the will of God, refused and rejected, and even upon the earth He had the attributes of omniscience. And today, if possible, we would like to restrain that knowledge of Jesus and limit His abilities. Jesus tells His disciples of that day and hour that no man knows, not even the angels which are in heaven, neither the Son but the Father only.

To stay the hand of God and delay the return of Christ; God not being a respecter of any person honors at will the intercessory prayers of the righteous. Jesus, being the Word, that Word has not come forth from the Father. The knowledge of that hour had not been determined because of the longsuffering, gracious mercy and goodness of God. Just as He proclaims before Moses, "The Lord God merciful, and gracious, longsuffering, and abundant in goodness and truth."

Because of this, Jesus continues to make intercessions for us daily. God is still honoring the intercessory prayers of the righteous, not willing that any should perish. It is the church's task to make the invisible kingdom of Christ visible, calling those things which be not as though they were. We stand before the gates of hell endangered of hell's fire. For the righteous scarcely enter heaven, and we question the knowledge of Jesus regarding a statement to His disciples. Must we continue to distinguish the two natures of Christ like Marcion?

Man does not know God, expired on the cross, and the universe did not cease to exist. The flesh died, but God is a spirit. We think that God is restricted to heaven, who allows His glory to spill over into our atmosphere. The kingdom of God is a present reality invisible to the world.

It is not at all surprising that the disciples imagined that the law had been cancelled. How tempting to suppose Jesus would put an end to the law of the old covenant that we may be free to enjoy the liberty of the Son of God. After all, we now possess all things through the sovereign grace of God. Jesus said we must not imagine that He has come to destroy the law or the prophets, so He vindicates the authority of the law of the old covenant. It becomes a new law only because it is Christ who binds us to it. Yet people think that they can cleave to Jesus and be free from the law.

The Lord's supper, the concept and reality is real, and yet frivolous and unnecessary if we try to read anything supernatural from it. Christ instituted a new way for remission of our sins. The ratification of the new covenant by the blood of Christ instituted during the last supper was the pouring out of the blood on the cross.

The old and the new covenant cannot be separated. Jesus did not come to destroy it, and God still exercises judgment in it, which brings us again to justification by faith. God so graciously accepts Christ's obedience to the covenant, because He accomplished what we are incapable of doing ourselves. But Jesus is not a substitute for our personal obedience that is required, for it cost His blood.

A will is of a higher authority. If freewill is the ability to make choices without prior influence, just say free choice. Twisting words is a trick of the devil with the intentions to cause people to stumble. Word games is a wicked and diabolical academic trick. To have free choice is to be able to choose according to our desire. Adam never had a free will. Adam had a free choice—freedom to choose right from wrong, obey or disobey—and his freedom of choice was not affected by the fall.

All of us have freedom of choice. However, what has been affected by sin is our ability to make the right choice. Choices are hard to make because there are consequences. If we make the wrong choice, it affects us; if we make the right choice, it affects us. Choice has power determined by us. Adam eats from the tree, and he uses his power of choosing to do so. God will not decide upon our actions. Our choice is not always God's will. Even the faculty of deciding what one will do is only reasoning awaiting the power of choice.

If God thought man had a will when he received the command not to touch, execution would not have been delayed, death would have been imposed the very day the transgression occurred. It is impossible for man to have a free will, because as soon as we create a will, it is found in direct opposition to God. This is what happened to Lucifer, and wickedness was found in him. Nevertheless, we consider these things contentions and striving about the gospel. They are for the most part unprofitable and vain. The end result is the choice to do what we want to do.

Reformed theology has shifted the focus from Christians to Calvinists. For them the gospel has become the gospel of predestination. How do the sophisticated and scholarly accept predestination except for selfish reasoning, for their own eternal security? Justification is a finished work of Christ. Whom God calls, He justifies through Christ. Salvation is a finished work, for it is up to man to put forth his hand and take.

Salvation only to the elect, a less loving God; some people have not the knowledge of the truth. God insures the salvation of all people when God planted the desire to know Him in the human heart. God has no pleasure in the death of him that dies. We must stop teaching that God is partial, who chooses some but not all. The blood is required at our hands. It is not a question to be disputed, but God gives all men the ability to come to Christ. We cannot change a person who does not want to be changed; that is their choice.

Let the Scriptures speak; that is the revelation. Having based much of our knowledge on Paul, we hold his doctrine as wholly trustworthy to describe the operations of God, who's commandments he refused to keep and refused the disciples' teaching. To place God on a mortal level and keep Him there in line with our ideas, rules, and principles, and make God's ways conform to our thinking, we provoke God to anger. Predestination is in fact not a biblical doctrine. It is not a true apostolic teaching. The gospel is not taking words from the Bible and reading in so deep that people drown, while we stand before the gates of hell.

Welcome to the gates! The gates of heaven or the gates of hell. The path of life or the path of death; inching closer to the edge or stretched out toward the sky; blinded to the call without any knowledge how to respond. Some people are so morally depraved that they resist the very presence of God. We blind ourselves to our own evil and to the grace which others are just as entitled to as we are. Any view of predestination is frightening. The deeper issue and horrible darker side of predestination is unfortunately people are destined for damnation. Our objective goal is to reach as many souls as possible with the gospel.

Predestination is dangerous because it profanes the word of *forgiveness*. The Word of God recognizes opposition when it meets it, and this is certainly a potent force. Reformation theology has separated from the rest of society. They put trust in their own works that gives them special rights and privileges, enjoying power and standards of judgments which qualifies them to exert a peculiar authority over others. They have adopted a superior attitude to pass unqualified condemnation on the rest of the world.

To try and grasp God's thoughts and persuade themselves and others that predestination is the will of God as if God is unfair. For Satan only thought to exalt himself; we tread on dangerous ground with the very thought that God is giving grace to one person and not equally to another. The undegenerated, unreached, and unelected are all made in the image and likeness of God. The greatest lesson from the greatest teacher is that all men are created equal, so love thy neighbor as thyself.

If we thought for one moment God has rejected one soul, we are deceived. We are not to claim for ourselves special privileges which we deny to others. We are to intercede for souls and stand in the gap. If Moses did not intercede for the children of Israel, if Jesus the high priest do not intercede for us today, if we do not intercede for others, then we have not learned the principle of "love thy neighbor."

Many people do not respond to the call, and many chosen do not understand their election. If God has chosen some people unto election and others unto rejection, it is the purpose of God to use the elect to show that there is no unrighteousness with Him. God has elected them to become mediators, conformed in the image and likeness of His Son, filled with the Holy Spirit to compel those who are in direct defiance to the will of God to come. But the elect are heady and high-minded above those that have been called because they are chosen. Insisting that God determined it to be this way when we have the power to persuade God through prayer. We have lost sight of our primary aim, which is to follow Christ, looking for the lost.

If God choose these elect, then God raised up these elect to show His power, like He did Pharaoh because of their deceitfulness, disobedience, and unwillingness to pluck those out of the fire who are presumed predestined to hell; that the purpose of God according to the election might stand. That God might show His power that His name might be declared in all the earth through these elect who so skillfully resist His will.

Who then are the vessels of wrath, and where are the vessels of mercy? The reverse effects of predestination are those that were invited and did not deserve to come. They did not deserve their election. As we scramble to fill the house with guests, our error in neglecting certain individuals, assuming that God predestined some people to everlasting life, and others to everlasting death would single us out without a wedding garment of righteousness, speechless without excuse bound hand and foot cast into outer darkness rejected. We are not to sit in judgment of our fellowman.

The narrow way is difficult to find and harder to tread. The truth is that there are only two ways to tread: the way of life and the way of death. Once either of these doors has been entered, there is no possibility of return. It is a fearful thing to fall into the hands of an angry God, but it is a dangerous and hurtful reality having accomplished nothing in this life that would glorify God, and if that wasn't enough, having been on the wrong path.

Chapter 7

HEAVEN OR HELL PART 2

Enter the Eternity

These things are written under heaven or hell because the doctrine that we choose will determine which door we will enter for eternity. Today we must understand the need for reform. It is not always easy to see where a legitimate school of thought ends and heresy begins. That is why a doctrine may be tolerated in one church and forbidden in another. Without a revelation, the Scriptures cannot be read or understood in the same spirit in which they were created.

An atonement has been made for every person's sins. People who are saved are those who respond to the call of the gospel with faith. The person who fails to embrace the saving work of Christ is not saved. The propitiation of the cross and the satisfaction of God's justice have absolutely nothing to do with our faith. (God is pleased with the cross, and because of that action, justice was satisfied.) The atonement produces the desired results apart from any faith we have;

neither is faith necessary for the satisfaction of *divine justice.* The work is finished! Faith present or absent in a sinner does not determine the results of Christ's work of satisfaction, which is complete in itself. Christ satisfied the demands of God for everyone, yet one by one each person must put forth their hand and take.

We shall be judged according to our own works. How shall we survive if we have not been trained to do good works? The atonement is still there it has not been voided or nullified. Our sins were paid for absolutely and unequivocally before we believed. Just because we don't come to Christ, it does not make His atonement incomplete. It is our faith that makes Christ's atonement sure to produce salvation in us. Christ's work in itself saves everyone and makes salvation possible. If no one believed the work of Christ, it is still there. If no one takes and eats from the tree of life, it is still there. If not one person believed on the brazen serpent Moses placed on the pole, as God had said, it was still there for the looking.

Today if we do not look up at the cross of Jesus Christ, the event is still there, the work of Christ is still complete. Justice is satisfied and accepted. Christ did not die in vain even if not one person was saved. Know that the love of God was shed abroad. God provides all that is necessary for salvation to make salvation for all possible, including the gift of faith. If God does not supply the means of faith, then we who are chosen ought to stand in the gap like Moses and plead for the salvation of the people in demonstration of our love toward all men. For God so loved the world.

The Bible is an instrument of salvation, but soon as it begins to only confirm and reinforce our own views, we are no longer extracting a message from the text but projecting our own message onto the words of the Scripture. A textbook knowledge of God is completely different than a spirit-filled knowledge of God. Wisdom that is from above is without partiality.

Most saints don't count the cost because we are taught that everything is free. We are taught that God's grace requires no cooperation from us; however, when the heart of the sinner is truly changed, we see the fruits of obedience. We must not try and exact order from behind a desk and expect a textbook to pour out instructions on righteous living. We are fighting spiritual wickedness; Satan is a defeated foe, but a foe indeed, a real opponent of war, and we must not forget his fury.

The doctrine that has spread like a wild fire promoting all kinds of insincere confessions of faith is aphorism; once saved, always saved. People run in under it looking for eternal security. This wisdom descended not from above, but is earthly sensual devilish, set on fire from hell. A person who has genuine faith and has come to true authentic saving faith and fall away from that faith can and will lose his salvation. When a righteous man turns from his righteousness and commit sin that he dies in his sins, all his righteousness which he has done shall not be remembered.

Positive assurance of perseverance is to commit to that which is lawful and right and turn away from wickedness after having received the grace of justification. Sin conceived brings forth death. There is no level of sin that is more offensive than another; all sin against God is equally offensive. Sin is so serious that we actually fall from salvation, because assurance does not guarantee perfection.

To think that God only expresses grief over sin, then can we better understand why the world is in the condition it is in today? If sin was such a casual matter, then Satan would still have his place in heaven. We make sin out to be such a light offense, because our view of God is so low and with a heightened look at self. Today assurance is a license for loose living. If we fall into sin and our conscience is seared, we know we have grieved the Holy Spirit and have wounded our walk with God. Assurance is to know that we can get back up after we have fallen and go boldly to the throne of grace seeking help in the time of need.

The abandonment of faith is what the reformed acknowledges as false assurance; however, if assurance does not guarantee perfection, then there is no purpose in the doctrine. If we sin after having received assurance, then we still subject ourselves to damnation. We must not believe that we cannot totally or finally fall away from the state of grace. Furthermore, it is not impossible for the elect to fall from grace. We both stumble and fall. Saved people fall into sin. It doesn't mean they have a false sense of salvation, or there was an abandonment of their faith. A just man falls seven times and rises back up again.

All Christians are assailed by doubt and uncertainty. It is no guarantee after we fall that we will have a chance to be reconciled to God. In fact, it is no guarantee that we are even still reconciled to God. Jesus never promised such securities, but through much tribulation we must enter in. People will make for security sake professions of faith and exhibit zeal for Christ confessing with their mouth, and what man can say that it was not genuine. Just because people disown their faith to death does not mean that they were not genuine. People need prayer and help, and this is where the road gets narrow. Because those who are saved are still vulnerable to sin and temptation attacks.

A true Christian who may sin can fall from grace even though God is holding onto them. It is our responsibility to hold fast to our faith. We have twisted the Word of God to acquire the highest achievement of Scripture exaggeration imaginable to justify the commandments of men.

Death is final, and we must get this in our spirit while we are still in the margin of life. Eternal union with God or eternal separation from God. Enter your eternity without banners or signposts we approach the other side of reality. Once entered there can be no returning, time is frozen, and it no longer flows; all work has ceased.

Death is not a mistake, a myth, or a fantasy, but a real spirit and hell follows, warning us of the dangers to disrobe. Repentance and renewal defeat the enemy, but half-truths and very small lies are the undetected unnoticeable road to hell, the gradual one. The small sins are the very ones which separate the sinner from God unknowingly. We not only say that the ways of the Lord are not equal. We teach that the ways of the Lord are not equal and detour true believers to a ditch. People fall away, and people are carried away by these doctrines of men.

Tomorrow's future is already today's past. It is heaven or hell; God or Satan. People were saved by the single historical fact of the resurrection and the single theological doctrine of redemption. The gospel was written not to make Christians, but to edify Christians already converted. People have used Christianity as means to their own advancement, and God will not be used as a convenience.

Battles have ensued over the correct version of the Bible. Battles have established certain books, accepted certain parts, and disclaimed others. Then people revised passages they considered indecent. Some replaced offensive sections with their own writings; some changed words and passages. There are those who have made thousands of alterations in material they considered indecent. Some made changes even in decent parts of the Bible, monopolizing the Bible's antiquity using it for power, and stand behind it as God's Word for authority using it to gain wealth, enslave, and terrify society with doctrinal order.

The purpose is not to deter any from following after Christ or reading the Bible, but we have completely made a mess of God's teachings. It is imperative for God to dig up His vineyard that has brought forth thorns and thistles. The enemy tries to deceive the whole human race all the time, trying to cut every generation off from all others by darkening our intellect. Because the danger is that the characteristic errors of one generation may be corrected by the characteristic truths of another.

God went through some drastic measures to stay in communion with man. Born in the flesh of the man·He created, projecting Himself into sin for us to be reconciled to Him. God is holy, who could not look upon sin, who could not be in the presence of Sin, could not identify with it. In fact, God had a different concept of sin, until He clothed Himself in sinful flesh and put all our sins upon Him.

Understand that God is unchanging, God never changes. He is exactly what He was before man. The same yesterday, today, and forever, and we cannot explain why God isn't any greater, because He is already as great as He could ever be and greater than we can ever imagine having conquered sin. All-knowing yet He knows no sin. He was touched with the feelings of our sin, but without sin, in all points tempted. Because knowing sin now adds nothing to God. Here is the *love of God*: He identified with sin for us.

This is why God is so angry and with the wicked every day. We trample truth to the ground. God removed the flaming sword that kept the way to the tree of life, and now hell is heated seven times hotter; heated because we are without excuse. We are not to compromise or make a truce with the devil. We are not to stand in agreement with the world. Everyone wants to secure their future, but the question remains: Where have we secured our eternity? In heaven or hell?

The sting of death, where we cease to exist, has been removed. We do not stay there; we enter into our eternity. How shall we enter the eternity, and why must we fear when Jesus holds the keys of death and hell? But we must still pass through those doors. Comforted or tormented, today we are faced with choices to choose right from wrong, good from evil, eternal life or eternal damnation. The choice we make determines our fate. What we do determines our future tomorrow. Passing through one channel of life to the next, there is a great gulf fix which, once we pass, we cannot return from there to here.

Beware, the trumpets blow. Death and hell roam mercilessly and have the power to inflict it. Deception is at an all-time high, the spirit of the Antichrist has taken on a new disguise. False prophets and false teachings acknowledge that Jesus has come in the flesh and is from God; behold, now they bear light, but no hope. They make the spirit of truth unrecognizable.

The Lamb of God has finished His work. We are being aligned with the will being done in heaven. The shift is in silence. How do we expect you to see the spirit of the living God, where angels are conducting the affairs? Word confirms the works were finished from the foundation of the world. It turns and continues exactly as we think it should, and we expect it will. It is unnecessary to seal this; it is the last warning.

This is for eternity. Some people have been hardened through the misleading and persuasiveness of sin through doctrines that are false. Our soul is at risk; our life is at stake. Let us wash our robes as if we are those that are in the great tribulation. We are the generation where we think we are on the narrow path, but the moment that the least of these words are found offensive, it proves the inability to know when God is speaking.

Be still and stand up. Reflect on those who have passed on, who have brought their prayers and presented them to God; while prayers are still approachable to God in the space of that half an hour. We will not delay the hand of God, and there is never another time where an angel stands at the altar before the throne and offers the prayers of the saints, the prayers with smoke of incense offered from the angel's hand to God. Get caught up with us and partake of a glimpse of this paradise, the eternal abode of God. Of the activities that take place in heaven, nothing is unpleasant. To be in the presence of the glory of God is great joy.

John wrote what he saw; he did not write all symbols or imagery, but what he saw. God wants us to see, but we are stubborn in our ways. We want God's Word to align with the way that we think, according to our reality, and the great work of God goes unnoticed.

John saw the angels, John saw the thrones, he heard the voices of many people. He saw the new heaven and the new earth. John saw the holy city, new Jerusalem, coming down from God out of heaven. The angel showed him these things. Heaven and all its scriptural imagery is not merely symbolical. We are to receive it as a little, teachable, and ever-learning child. The timelessness and preciousness can be expressed as gold, but we need to take God at His Word.

God gives us a glimpse as He pulls back the veil to see the significance of what appears on earth, the reality of what is and is to come as we stand at the brink of eternity. We have entered the unknown where it is less likely to see the good pleasures of God. In fact, why would God give away His good pleasures now, a reward that last forever in a world that is temporary? The things of God are kept from our view, within our grasp, but out of our reach.

Set our minds on things above, advancing the kingdom, anticipating the glories of heaven, gripped by the powers of the coming age, united with God in eternity, sharing His splendor and power. For what good is it to say that we are on the Lord's side after He cracks the sky and walk on stage, then life is over, and we enter the eternity.

But consider Satan briefly. We find him rearing his head in the heavens. Satan fell and has still been on the scene. When this life is over, we are found being accused by Satan before God. There is indeed life after death, heaven or hell, the splendor and vastness with the anticipation to bear the image of the heavenly man. The second man is not flesh and blood, and except we be born of the spirit, we cannot so much as see, much less enter into the kingdom of God.

Do you hear the voice of the bridegroom? The sound of a trumpet. This is meat as we witness the blaze of His glory, the fire of His judgment for a moment, briefly. People live in fear of death and what might lie beyond in time and space, because most people do not have a personal relationship with or have relational knowledge of God. God sits on His holy throne, in His holy habitation against the twelve gates of the city.

But consider death, and nothing followed, not even the extension of life. No immortality, we just cease to exist. The breath that made man a living soul goes back to the giver. Like a flower that fades away or a candle snuffed out, we just die.

There is no function, no memory, no senses. Never to give account to some of the deeds done in this life where people could live like they want. People think this and live their life to the full, and that is their choice; they think that they are in the land of the living going to the land of the dead. When in reality we are in the land of the dead and dying headed for the land of the living, and we are blinded to it.

We never consider the complexity of our bodily components and the intricate design and genetic makeup it took to make us who we are. There is a lot of creative work behind the created man, and we take it for granted as if life really cease to exist. The books are opened; the court is seated. The dead small and great stand before the great white throne.

It is wise to consider and ponder some of the many reasons why God teaches us to love everybody. Man looks at the outer appearance and passes judgment according to what he sees. Our outlook must be transformed, so God brings us to a place of love on earth first.

Take a look at Satan: sinister, destructive, and hateful. Most people when they see his godhood, after they have shined a light on him, fall in love and start to worship him, reasoning that his ways are not that bad, considering that they make perfectly good sense. "Save for the future and live for tomorrow," logic that kicks truth to the ground. A light might be to our amazement and bewilderment to see a god and almost the most beautiful creature in all of heaven. Prominent in the world affairs, master of the natural laws of the universe, allowing us to walk on in the imagination of the mind.

Christ connects us to the eternal world beyond this present life. God controls all aspects of the universe: time, space, matter, power, and motion. Jesus was never confined by our limitations of time and space as people assumed having flesh and bone. Yet we must never take anything from our earthly existence, no matter how good or noble the reality may seem, and apply it to the things of God.

We rarely give others a glimpse of what life will be like in eternity. It is important to understand that any former activity in this life will be done away with. A sense of gratitude should fill our hearts as we thank the Father who has made our citizenship in the kingdom of heaven possible. Our character must reflect the principles and practices of the kingdom of God. It is our responsibility to conform to the image and likeness of Christ, His culture, and His character. As citizen's heaven-bound, our behavior and attitudes should reflect a person who is already transferred into the kingdom of heaven, where the activities are live and worship is real. Love is required; this must be an essential aspect of our character.

We are invited to the marriage supper of the lamb, and the feast is at hand. We have been called and did not come. Prepared is a dinner with love and herbs. This word does not bear fruit when it is understood, only when it is applied. Everyone does that which is right in his own eyes. This is the marriage the King made for His Son, and all things are ready.

For those who do not like temple worship, who despises fellowship, and do not like to pray, heaven is not your place. Heaven is a true place for worship and adoration. The dowry has been paid with precious blood. This is that blood that purified the heavens, now appearing in the presence of God for us. In the twinkling of an eye, we are swept up to this high plateau of spiritual life. The veil is drawn aside, and the eyes of man peer into the mysteries of heaven, seeing with the eyes of God, things as they really are. Yet we still live as though we share the same delusion and disappointment as the world. We live as if redemption has changed nothing.

This is not some kind of religious fantasy. The breath that God has given us will never leave us. We belong to God. Where shall we flee from His presence, when His presence is His very breath in us? Life does not cease to exist. God loves us, and we ignore this. This preparation process is our rehearsal, and there are no second chances. God does not want us to get comfortable in this earth, and His promise of heaven is not here and now. We struggle to keep our attention on the world to come because there is no encouragement for us to accept heaven as a natural continuation of our existence.

Enter the eternity through the gateway to the abyss, the entrance into eternal damnation, hell created for the devil and his angels. We find there people who reject God, swallowed up. It is not the rejection that is displeasing to God, for there are thousands upon thousands who attend to God and ten thousand upon ten thousand that bow down and worship before Him. The anger of the Lord is against sin. Fire from the Lord has burned from the beginning now confined to a place of terror. A fire is kindled. God is provoked with anger. Jesus came out of the grave to taste for us. We assume it is beneath the earth since the ground split apart, and the earth opened its mouth and swallowed Korah and those who rose against Moses and went down alive into the realm of the dead. The earth closed over them that believed not. The reality is hell is a real place, and hell has enlarged itself above measure.

This ought to fuel our passion to see lost souls come to Christ. Locusts with human faces running toward those coming teeth like lions biting and tails with stingers striking like scorpions, the unimaginable wails and screams. Everlasting punishment is perpetual, never ending. A dark realm sensual demonic without any pleasure. Sheol exchanged for sinful choices. Choked by smoke, burning hate, hurting sounds of dead people crying in torment.

We must consider what kind of existence awaits us when we escape this body of death by death. We all have slumbered and slept. Even the wise virgins awakened by a sound, "Behold, the bridegroom is coming," and it has caught us completely by surprise. The terror will fill people who thought they were eternally secure. People do not want Christ to return and have *no* expectation whatsoever in His return; not because they think their deeds are evil, but the pleasures of this life have made many comfortable.

We are listening for a sound. What God is doing simply does not fit the world's expectations of what they are predicting. And what will be the sign? That is the dilemma. We anticipate a second coming of King Jesus. Experts say that they are positive of what to expect, but the events do not fully register while they are still unfolding. We expect everything will occur in one unbroken sequence, but with the rod of His mouth and the breath of His lips, we hear this great sound of a trumpet.

The Lord is warning, urging people to be prepared for a time of tribulation. It belongs to the end of the age. We fall between the rapture and the return where things progress and grow worst. Souls leave their bodies daily causing tragedy and great disaster, caught up. Those left behind are puzzled and saddened by the tragedy. But you say, why can't we see this? But you did from a natural standpoint and not a spiritual one.

"What went ye out to see?" Our vision has to come from God, and our perception must be spiritual. It took ten years for the earth to reach the planet Pluto, an indication of how high heaven is from earth. Souls die daily, they disappear, and we are left behind. Most people don't want to die. We are taught to love ourselves and cling unto life. But the disciples loved not their bodies unto death. Self-love is refusing to surrender all to Christ. Stop trying to get comfortable in this life. We should be living in expectancy ready to go at any moment. Oh, but this has been relatively mild. The fullness of the Gentiles has come.

Pay close attention to Israel how tribulation has begun. This will become relentless, faster, and louder as the time approaches, nearer, closer, quickly creeping in like a thief. This tribulation is so evil because it goes unnoticed almost until it is right up on us. The destructive forces of evil are in full operation and unleashed. We must not wait until we get to heaven to see heaven's perspective. Fear God and give glory to Him, for this is the hour. Disaster strikes quick. The Pharisees and scribes understood the prophecy well, with all its signs, and they simply missed the Messiah. People draw their own conclusion and walk in the blindness of their imagination to destruction because nothing fits their assumptions. Jesus did not fit their interpretation. We set our minds into thinking certain thing must happen a certain way and find ourselves missing the move of God.

Chapter 8

RELATIONSHIP WITH GOD

The earth is not full of the knowledge of the Lord. As we look back through the centuries, from the apostolic times until the present hour, we have approached the Laodicea age, where we have begun to abandon our religious faith. We are neither on fire for God or completely turned hostile to God. Because of this, we can now begin to see the rapture taking place. Lost groups of Christianity reformed or suppressed now live within the church. Our founded belief is beginning to be lost by sharing these diverse beliefs, sharing and accepting ideas contrary to sound doctrine agreeing and compromising with deception.

We digress from our progress persistence on various alternative forms of Christianity. We must anoint our eyes with eye salve that we may see. And how do you suppose we buy gold from God? For a relationship with God, the worldviews are to be rejected. As Christianity moves to refine or redefine its theological views, they lose the basic principles of simplicity. As we reflect on truth to be cherished, being in error carries great eternal consequences.

Relationship with God: The Approach

Christians today compromise instead of condemn, expressing freedom of choice instead of abiding in our religious traditions. If we seek truth and understand the way Scripture was formulated, direct revelation from God takes precedence. There is a greater fascination for a diverse manifestation of religious expressions even though some beliefs and practices bring damnation.

This is not the time nor the hour to bite and devour one another. Satan is loose, and we are being trampled. Times have changed, and we are a threat to our own existence by not approaching God. The whole world wanders after a false sense of hope that guides our actions and influence a behavior that leads to eternal torment.

For a personal relationship with God, we must reach higher ground. This is the type of approach that puts God before us, our wisdom beside us, our words beneath us, and our thoughts behind us. Salvation is dependent upon our relationship with God; Christ bridges the gap to God by His blood, and we stand before God righteous through Christ.

A relationship with God is precious, powerful, and worth every effort. We are told to go boldly to the throne of grace, but if we do not consider who it is that we approach, then yes, it is an act of boldness. For holy is the Lord God Almighty, the only wise God, eternal, immortal, invisible, high, and lifted up. This is the God who created the universe who belongs glory, majesty, dominion, and power seated and dwelling in light unapproachable. In obedience we turn to God and are accepted, and the real contact begins as we approach the living God to commune, fellowship, and build a relationship with Him.

Many Christians stand in spiritual stagnation because they do not approach God. It is difficult to approach God without communication, but approaching God is more than just prayer. What is impossible to us by nature we must gain through the spirit of grace for this union with God in love and spirit to exist. Genuine obedience reveals genuine love toward Him, and we have failed to reach the expectations required of us by God, to glorify God as He ought to be glorified. We draw breath to return to Him in prayer, praise, and adoration, and failure to glorify God, refusal to acknowledge and honor Him perverts the very reason for our existence.

All the royal province knows that any man or woman who approaches the king in the inner court without being summoned, the king has but one law, that they be put to death, unless the king extends the gold scepter to them and spare their life.

The queen put on her royal robe and stood in the inner court of the palace in front of the king's hall without being summoned. Clothed in a robe of righteousness, the king was sitting on his royal throne in the hall facing the entrance. When he saw the queen standing in the court, he was pleased with her and held out to her the gold scepter that was in his hand. So the queen approached and touched the tip of the scepter.

How much greater is the heavenly king, the King of kings, than this earthly king? Many times we come into the presence of the great and holy God, approaching the magnificent splendor of the God of the universe, without being summoned, filthy, with shoes on our feet, and we make light of it, expecting that because His mercy endures forever, He will hold out His kingly golden scepter and ask, "What is thy request?"

Jesus Christ, the righteous, passed through the heavens and stands before God as an advocate, but there is a process to the approach and there is a relationship to be had with God. It is true we have confidence to draw near to the throne of grace by reason of our merciful and faithful high priest. But do we always approach with thanksgiving and enter His courts with praise? Are we always thankful to Him? Yet people often wonder why prayers go unanswered.

Nadab and Abihu approached God and offered a strange prayer before the Lord, a *fire* contrary to his command, and fire came out from the presence of the Lord, and they died. We must be careful when approaching God. The children of Israel could not even approach the mountain where God was or touch the foot of it. Moses could not approach or enter the tent of meetings because the glory of the Lord filled the tabernacle.

When approaching the *true and living God* with prayers, take caution. God is in heaven, and we are on earth. There will never be a person so pure or so deeply immersed in loving God who does not approach Him in this life totally absorbed, yearning for a deeper knowledge and a deeper love from Him. And God does not extend the golden scepter and asks, "What is thy request?" The Lord God is pleased with such a sacrifice.

Specific regulations governed every approach to Jehovah. He was accessible only on a certain day, by means of certain ordinances, and then only to the high priests. But when God became flesh and the veil was torn, anyone can enter into the holiest by the blood of Jesus. Having the boldness to enter into the holiest, we are now having difficulty drawing near with a true heart.

The theologian after death was given the choice between going to heaven or going to a lecture on heaven, and he chose the lecture—

knowledge over experience. We are concerned about when Christ is coming, instead of being ready when He comes. The approach is love in action; to fall in love with the idea of approaching God instead of doing the actual work is one and the same. It takes experience to approach God, because God must be worshipped.

We talk about a closer walk with God, but the angels rejoice and hasten to assist us, yet we do nothing to move closer. And having done all to stand, we must now progress. We put on the whole armor of God: girt with the truth, with the breastplate of righteousness, feet fit with peace, shield of faith, the helmet of salvation, and equipped with the sword of the spirit. And many Christians just stand there never understanding that the gold scepter has been outstretched. God is pleased with the work of Christ, but they never approach Him.

Satan's war tactics are intensifying, and we must take part in this spiritual war instead of waiting for Satan's next move to take us out. To know God, we must build a relationship with Him. God knows us, but we must get to know Him. To build a relationship, we must approach Him. We cannot just stand there and literally do not move, almost useless because spiritual movement is made by prayer.

We approach God with prayer, we commune with prayer, we meet with God in prayer, and we are only active with prayer. Praying always with all prayer and supplication in the spirit is part of God's armor. We say that there is only one way to approach God, but that is not true. Jesus said that He was the way; He didn't say that it was the only way, but He said those who comes to God any other way is a thief and a robber. There is only one way accepted into the presence of God, and that is through the blood of Jesus Christ, the righteous one.

Many will say in that day, "Lord, Lord, haven't I done many works in thy name?" But He will answer and say, "I know you not. All this time you have been standing in my presence, and you never took time to approach me correctly. Of course I never knew you in a relationship."

A relational knowledge is different than knowledge of principles and processes; to know someone, you must meet them and spend time with them. To pray is the first step of knowing God. We dig out the promises of God like hidden treasures, reaping benefit after benefit through Christ, and we never turn to the giver to approach Him sincerely.

Ultimately, when we attempt to approach God, our reality is that we build sanctuaries for God to dwell among us. The temple was the visible symbol of God dwelling in our midst. Then we ignore His presence. We will not even take off our shoes in His presence. Then and when in the presence of God, as if it is a light thing, we disregard our position because of sin. We do not realize the magnitude of our closeness with the creator of the universe, enjoying unbroken fellowship, so easily broken.

Jesus at the brink of death, soul exceeding sorrowful, blood drops oozed to the ground. He could have called a multitude of angels to His rescue. "Father, is there any other way to save this lost world?" That was the cup; it was not all that physical suffering, but the spiritual torture of forfeiting the communion, fellowship, and relationship with His Father.

Understand the significance of why Christ's return is affected by prayer and why it is important to approach God with prayer for a relationship. Because when there is no one left to pray and intercede for the people, the results of the lack of prayer cause God to pour out

His indignation upon us and consume us with the fire of His wrath because of our sins. Prayer is so vital. God seeks to avoid judgment; He longs to spare us, but without intercessory prayer, the judgment God wishes to withhold must come.

Prayer is the approach. Prayer is a link, a lifeline that connects to those who would otherwise be hopeless. Prayer bears up the helpless ones to link the destitute with God. This is the importance of magnifying the approach to God. We are told that the principal thing is to stand before God, but if we were in a place with access to an exalted person, we would want to get up-close and personal with them. We don't just stand in their presence. So too with God. We must get up-close and personal with Him and just get familiar with God. He is more than an exalted person; He is the creator of the universe.

Prayer is conversation with God, and not all prayer is in words. Prayer goes beyond words. God prefers the heart without words. Once prayer has been established, and we have fully approached God, then can we intercede like Moses. Everyone will not be able to get in the presence of God; many will fail. We fail over and over again because we begin with our attention on God, and after a little while, we realize that we have not been focused on God at all. We start fantasizing or falling asleep or worrying about other things; distractions turn us away from the ultimate purpose of prayer: to get to know God.

We must first want it and seek it because of who He is. The love of God makes us want to know Him, and knowledge of God makes us love Him. If we rely on anything else besides faith to approach the presence of God, we will fail. God can do everything without our prayers, but He desires to show mercy. And when we pray for others, we show mercy, and mercy rejoices in mercy.

Implementing effective prayer falls entirely upon us. When the final prayers ascend before God, as the deadline approaches, we must pray for the salvation of others with the assurance that they will be saved.

Why does God save some people and not others? It is not because God is powerless. In fact, it's just that some people are the subjects of powerful and believing intercession while others have no one to pray for them. This means that no soul is saved apart from intercession. No one can come to God except the Father draws him, and the Father always draws by means of His spirit. Every soul who is saved is saved because someone has prayed for them and would not give them up to Satan. God desires for all men to be saved. He has made provision for the salvation of all. God takes no pleasure in the death of them that died. God makes provision for the salvation of the whole world.

This salvation is affected by intercession or lack of it. We somehow miss this spiritual truth, thread throughout the whole Bible, and never seem to teach this principle. If we do not intercede, then the Holy Spirit cannot do the work of convicting. The believers hold the balance of power, not only in the world affairs, but in the salvation of individual souls one by one.

The tongue has the power of life and death; therefore, by intercession or lack of it, we hold the power of life or death over the souls of sinners. Sinners need a sponsor, for we reach people one by one. This is why some people are powerfully convicted and converted while others are lost.

These are our weapons of war, mighty through God. We spend so much time praying for ourselves and not for others because we are painfully dissatisfied with our level of contact with God. We must not be deceived by thinking that God only sees believers. God is displaying His perfection to rescue us from our ignorance. What awakens His wrath is the inability to find believers to intercede on behalf of others. We should be grateful that God has wrought an intimate union between us and Him.

Most people do not know God with experience. Our approach to God is an approach to the problems of Christian living. People who know God are people who pray, stand firm, and take action. The approach is not the concept of physical distance; near or far it is more an experience understood through our personal relationship.

Faith is a belief system that believes on Him who we cannot see, nor do we know. Coming to know God more intimately and with a deeper understanding removes the barriers. We are brought into a relationship with God, and we are considered His family. Therefore, knowing God is more than knowing about Him.

As God's presence becomes real, His promises become real. If we don't trust God, it is because we don't know Him. And if we don't know God, it is because we don't trust Him enough to interact with Him personally. No Christian is refused the blessing of such experience, so no one will be exempt from its responsibility. Sin exerts a force that pulls us away from our intimacy with God. The nearer we become and the closer God comes to us, the more sensitive to sin we are made, and our sinfulness becomes clearer. It is love that desires to draw near to us, and the approach must be met with love.

To become true worshippers of God, we must always keep our eyes on God and His glory in all we do for perfect consciousness of His presence. It is important that we get alone and draw near to God and listen to Him speak to our hearts. We must renounce everything for the love of God. He is jealous in a sense that He wants our undivided attention, meaning everything that could take away the thought of God. This is worship, and it keeps us in His presence. Approaching God is difficult, and without faith there can be no approach to God.

As we reestablish the relations which existed from the foundation of the world, we must adjust our lives accordingly and stop trying to modify God. The grand passport into the presence of God is the blood of Jesus Christ to approach Him completely. Prayer is the most authentic form of worship, and intercession is totally unselfish because we show our love for others by bringing them into the presence of God, and this is the whole law.

Our only means of returning our communion to God is through prayer; it is the only real action. We must evidently realize that prayer has a big part in bringing prophecy to pass. Many conflicts rage constantly in the spiritual realm because prayer has no space or geographical limitations. The sense of spiritual well-being that comes from a right relationship with God is priceless.

Prayerlessness and lack of persistence equals ineffective prayer. Prayer must take on a deeper meaning. We must develop the habit of continual conversation with God. We must recognize God's presence within us and speak to Him at every moment. There should never be an idle moment or an idle mind where we are not worshipping God. We are made in the image and likeness of God, but we have absolutely no idea what that image looks like. And we must not think of God existing in our image; that is the way to remain ignorant of God completely.

The essential accuracy and truthfulness to the reality of God is in silent, intimate conversations with God, then we will begin to advance in the knowledge of Him. We must establish ourselves in the presence of God by continually communing with him. If we break away and start to commune with the world, it is hurtful and shameful to God. The look of the world is contagious and turns the slightest viewer into stone. Death strikes all who look to follow its ways. God is to remain the center of our attention. Evil begins in our thoughts, so we must reject them as soon as they become evident. It is difficult sustaining a spirit of prayer, constantly rejecting stray thoughts to only fall back into them. We must, in spite of all the difficulties, keep calling our thoughts back to God.

Prayer should be understood as including any form of communion or attempted communion with God, whether vocal or purely mental, affirmative and invocatory prayer, meditation, or the highest of all forms of prayer, contemplation. We do not have to be constantly in church to be with God; we do not need to shout out loud as He is closer to us than we think. Furthermore, do not pray aloud too much, hold yourselves before God, mute, unable to talk, keeping your mind from straying because it withdraws with the slightest distraction.

It is not enough to love God and to know Him only by a book, this is knowledge. We must make our faith alive, for without faith it is impossible to please God; this is experience. Extensive knowledge pleases man, but a faithful and obedient heart pleases God because knowledge without experience is vain. A relationship with God has to be experienced.

The approach is to things invisible. How do we even attempt to share this precious holiest walk without permission? It is secret. Information is limited. There are no resources available that can disclose a constricted isolated communion with God. It is conceived when we approach Him; it is birthed in the shadows of death, and it follows us into eternity. There is nothing to be told, yet we find glimpses of those who God allowed to leave a legacy that allows us to peek into their life to see the thoughts and intents of the heart; what worship consists of and what is acceptable. A relationship with God can never be learned. It must be experienced.

There is no method to holiness. The only procedure to a right relationship with God is to approach; it is a lifestyle. So narrow and rigid is the spiritual relationship with God that it builds a bridge between the visible and invisible. Anything that would thwart such an alliance, anything that would keep us ignorant to close fellowship with God, is greatly encouraged by spiritual wickedness. The relationship with God is so important, and people do not put forth any effort to relate to God. They just go through the motions. We must serve God for better or for worse.

Our greatest spiritual asset is a habitual consciousness of the actual presence of God. He is always with us in actual presence, and this should be our realization. Legions of angels encamp around us and we think that they are surrounding us to protect us, but they are attending to the mighty God who is in us as He communes with us. God must be the center of our thoughts, deeper than any thought. When our mind is free, we should turn it to God—silent or aloud, alone or in a crowd, anywhere, easily and naturally, as a friend—and His presence will become real.

This is an absolute unconditional surrender of ourselves unto the fullness of God. The approach is to surrender to God's complete indwelling, living habitually on a high plane of close fellowship with God. He wants to be our life and do His work through us using us, and our works are the results of His life in us.

Now consider spiritual relationships. There are some people closer to God than others, because there are diversities of relationships but in the same spiritual approach. There are differences of administrations to those relationships, being many, yet we are all partakers of the same form of worship dwelling in light unapproachable. It is the same God which works all in all. Relationships are given to every man to profit.

Each relationship is constant communion and fellowship, and all these relationships with God, the creator of the universe, are working through the same approach. Some are professional relationships while others are more intimate. It is dangerous to even consider what we do for God. In fact, it is what God does for us that we must take into account. Just as offering a sacrifice of praise to God is our moral responsibility, so, too, our approach to God is our spiritual responsibility. It is a mental approach; our minds must reach out toward God with outward obedience of this inward fellowship.

Consider Satan again, gone to and fro throughout the earth with no hindrance, freely moving, marching unhindered and unchallenged in the earth. But there is one place where he has no foothold, where his power is unrecognized, and that is in our hearts and mind. Satan cannot read our thoughts. This is why silent prayers is such an effective deadly weapon. Satan considers our ways; our sinful flesh is the book that he diligently reads. Satan cannot see into the minds of any, and he watches to see how we respond to the information that he has planted. A quiver of hell's arrows stored until the time comes to prove the bow which Satan will shoot them to get an advantage over us.

Prayer is one of the most difficult exercises we will ever undertake, because in our prayers we insist on trying to talk to God in our distorted attempts to worship him, but be still; God wants to talk to us. We are uneasy and negative about the mention of meditation, and some people think such practices can open the door to evil activities that can lead to misguided conclusions. But meditation is a means of communion with God. It is holy thoughts in the presence of God with the help of God to increase our knowledge of Him. We conjure up images of people sitting in a position engaging in trance-like activities. The act of meditation is a prayer of a higher calling, a spiritual exercise.

It is very hard to concentrate and bring our thoughts into the presence of God. We must remove anything from our hearts so that God may reign there unchallenged. The way to a deeper knowledge of God is to surrender, renunciation of self. Possessive clinging to things is one of the most harmful habits in life. This is not recognized as evil, for it is natural, but it is evil.

As sinners returning to the presence of God, we enter, offer the blood, pass through the veil, with the light of the world, eat the bread of life, offer unceasing prayer, and still have not entered into the presence of God. Yet there is another veil separating the sinner from the presence of God. This last veil was rent, opening the way for every worshipper in the world to come straight into God's divine presence. God is waiting for us to push forward to conscious awareness of His presence, and not positional but actually, and behind that last veil is God. We must seek if haply we might feel after Him and find Him though He is not far.

The highest love of God is not intellectual, but spiritual. God is a spirit, and only a spirit can worship Him and really know Him. So with the veil removed by the sacrifice of Jesus, why do we tarry without? We must not be envious when we see others come straight into God's divine presence. This is a beautiful gift for souls who are determined to follow God.

Millions of Christians do not know God on a personal level. They don't think of God as being knowable. God is not real to people who are trying to love an idea or be loyal to a principle. God waits for our response to recognize His presence, then the eternal world will come alive. God is here when we are aware of His presence and when we are unaware of it. God made man a living soul with a spirit to commune with the spiritual world, and we need a fuller awareness of spiritual realities with a greater desire for the things of God.

For this relationship to blossom we need to break down whatever barriers that exist to keep God away from certain zones of our life. When we sin, God withdraws from us and allows us to experience the unholy act on our part. God suspends the relationship to demonstrate an unwillingness to become an accomplice in our sins. God withdraws and leaves us to our fate until we recognize the truth of what we have done and take the initial steps to repair the damage, then the relationship resumes.

God will not speak before we are ready, and we must be in a position to listen. There is a lot of healing to be found in silence. We must assign to the spiritual world a higher priority because of God's spiritual nature. God with His words spoke, and things came into existence. We undermine the power of spoken word, yet we bless God and curse man with the same tongue. It is impossible to worship God with outer expressions, and to please Him we must use an inner expression. But since God has come in the flesh, He is able to identify with our fleshly worship.

If we want to go higher, learn to pray in the spirit, in silence. The heart glows with intense desire of our inner being speaking out in silence with the abundance of our grief and complaint. Hannah poured out her soul before the Lord God. She spoke in her heart. Only her lips moved, but her voice was not heard. She prayed in the spirit.

People really want to touch God and feel His love; they want to know what they cannot see. This is our ultimate goal, a relationship with God, and we are taking steps in approaching Him. God is a spirit, and He is invisible. Let our mind rest in the awareness of God; love and praise God for what He is in Himself. We must be bound to God spiritually to achieve by grace what is beyond us by nature, and if we are seeking God alone, we will not rest with anything less than God.

Chapter 9

THE CHURCH

The true and sincere worship of God according to His holy will and commandments are often profaned and neglected by many who do not keep holy the Lord's day but, in a disorderly manner, use many unlawful exercises and pastimes upon the Lord's day to the great scandal of the Christian faith.

Eleventh-century Christian writers inspired by God clearly brought forth revealed truth exposing the slightest sin to keep the church progressing under the apostolic tradition. The church, however, scrutinized everything, and anything that opposed the church was brought under persecution. It was difficult to write messages. Everything was done in secret because of the Pope. Messages were concealed, hidden in code, sometimes behind mythology, and even then consider heresy and banned.

The church was undergoing a strange transformation, and the role it played was sending people to hell causing men to sin unknowingly with its doctrines, and not much has changed.

Let us look back through the centuries, at the marks of the professing church from the apostolic times: the first love church with its decline, the suffering church under Roman persecution, the worldly church issued at the conversion of Constantine, the church when Rome was at its greatest power, the Reformation Church, who returned to the Word of God, and the Apostate Church of these last days where we see the abandonment of the Christian faith.

We have reached in this age, a time where we can begin to see the rapture taking shape. Our Lord gives the promise to keep us from the hour of tribulation that the whole world will experience, and this is that hour. Today we are wealthy with unbroken success, increasing with goods, and we need nothing. The only way that a person can be kept from this hour is to be taken out of the world when the hour strikes. There are no longer any shepherds, no one to led the flock to fresh waters, no one to protect us from the wolf. Today we are again condemning sinners without lifting a finger to help them. The hour has come to be fetched home to the kingdom of God.

If we do not refrain from work on the seventh day, God will refer to His own act of creation which He spent six days making the world before resting on the seventh day. And with the Lord, a day is as a thousand years, and a thousand years is one day. Therefore, six thousand years, if referred to a period of six days in which God has been actively involved with us people, then no matter how we view things, this is the seventh day.

Nothing can be more ruthless than to make people think that there is still plenty of time to mend their ways. The danger lies in the judgment of God, not in the death of the body, but in the eternal destruction of the soul. Eternity is long, and time is short. The terrifying fact in all of this is that God will withdraw His hand and reconciliation will no longer be possible.

The ability to know and decipher what path to take has become difficult to distinguish. The way people live would likely indicate that there is some other way to a relationship with God. Look at all the denominational families, national organizations, nondenominational, and various denominational divisions. Every kingdom divided against itself will not stand.

The church, which is the bride, is composed of many people throughout many generations. This is the real church spread out through time and space, rooted in eternity, and this church is invisible composed of all the redeemed of all ages. Christ has one bride, many members, but one body. The mystical union that is between Christ and the church does not rest on one generation. There is much complacency and error from people not knowing the Scriptures.

The church today is a historical institution, a big business, legal and intelligent, which gives credit to man's capacities and capabilities and praises man's achievements. The church has contributions in the hundreds of millions. The pleasures, luxury, and greed, the politics and worldliness. The church has become rich and powerful spreading like a green bay tree. Synthetic Christians and professional pastors use mass psychology setting themselves up as lord over God's heritage ruling their congregations for filthy lucre.

We are taught that tithes are fundamental to Christianity, or are tithes fundamental to church growth? We are competing for growth. It is no mystery why we cannot reach lost souls, refusing to ordain ministers who lack college training. The gospel is true and we are safe, but will you sin and then come and stand before God in a house which bears His name and say, "We are safe?" Safe to do what?

All these detestable things. Evolution of Christianity over time has changed and has introduced novelties and innovations, doctrines and practices into the church contrary to Apostolic teachings.

It is imperative to emphasize Bible revisions, because there was never a reason to overlook or correct the King James Version for the sake of trying to get a better understanding or explanation. The Holy Spirit will teach us all things and interpret hard-to-understand scriptures and passages. A word makes a big difference in the Word of God. It can pervert the whole text. Everyone wants to translate, creating more than one interpretation. These actions have hindered our advancement of the kingdom of God on earth. For almost four hundred years we read the Bible and it has not changed, and before that, it was one thousand years, and now we must relearn it all over.

We inquire of God and forget what we are told. Do not tempt God just to make our lives long and prosperous. God has given us His Sabbaths as a sign between us and Him, so we would know that it is He that made them holy, and we have utterly violated the sanctity of His Sabbath converting them to evil uses. It is time for God to act with all the violence and injustice, Satan with his deception, and the Antichrist.

This is for those who beat the way out before us, the travelling church, the worldwide missionary movement, the extension of Christ's kingdom represented by those early true missionary pioneers. It was a season of darkness with missionary heroism and daring exploits. The dangers, the wars, and barbarism of uncivilized people. The difficulties, the language barriers, the tension, bitter arguments, and ill-feelings toward denominations, doctrine traditions, and reform.

The godly desire of Bible-believing Christians who seriously took the words of Christ literally and obediently. They were traveling far distances around the globe even to the point of death all for the life and mission of the church. The things that today's Christians never come to appreciate in this millennium are the spiritual battles waged to bring us to this present day of salvation and the gospel of Christ Jesus. The establishment of the church and a deep-seated concern to carry to those who would otherwise never know the command to make disciples of all nations.

The apostles have passed on and have passed down the commission. The church has carried the torch through time faithfully. There was so much suffering in the lives of the people who have paved the way. The uncivilized cultures of the world were brought spiritual salvation and are now civilized. Today if we debate about the fate of those unevangelized souls who have never heard about Christ, then we are debating the wrong topic. This is a dangerous time we are living in, and the zeal and sense of urgency to the call continues.

The greatest prospect and fulfillment is that the gospel of the kingdom of God has been preached throughout the whole world; that is, when the end will come, and we are here. Who would ever expect that we would see this age come upon us? But it has; it is real, it is serious, and it is extremely dangerous. Each segment of time had their share of spiritual war and persecution. We assume that we are trouble-free, a time of spiritual prosperity. However, it is still necessary to preach the gospel to the world; the Great Commission is still in effect. The reformation and recovery of proper doctrine has passed, and the church has taken shape. We should be thankful for the saving grace of God who has allowed us to be civilized. Many of these pioneers did not get to see the fruits of their labors and these accomplishments; therefore, we must keep the flame burning.

Literacy is at an all-time high, so our goals should be more spiritual by understanding what we read. Blending Christianity with modern culture is courting disaster. We have lost focus of the true purpose of the church, and it is not selfpreservation. Modern civilization is a continued challenge to Christian faith. Technological innovations, mass consumerism, and intellectual status are leaving less concern for the lost souls. Raising tolerance to the highest level of virtue until it spills over into acceptance, and this is what we call advancement of new knowledge.

Children, we are not to compromise, make a truce, or agree with Satan. We are not to stand in agreement with the world. Satan is still the ruler of this world, and we see the world standing together. Not everyone will be enlightened and accept the Christian faith. In this millennium Satan reigns, and his objective is to keep us ignorant, distracted, and deceived with little sins unchecked while ungodliness is spreading throughout the land. Today the church has a long past and a short future. We have sounded the alarm; the trumpet is blowing; the watchman sees the sword coming.

The majority of the world's Christian leaders are White, Western, affluent, and capable. We see the invisible racial lines that divide the populace. Where God has called shepherds, men have made shepherds of themselves.

God has not made any rulers or leaders, so it is affluence that has bought the prestige and position. Now affluent, and in a club or organization, most people do not fit into that circle, where went all the believers with one heart and one mind who shared everything. If a person does not have certain degrees or have attended certain schools, most leaders are looking down. Why does the pew always have to be looking up, when we should be all equal? Reaching down, reaching up, everybody should be read as a peer. This is the shoddy thinking that infects so many minds.

Everybody that has ever been used by God has suffered greatly to some degree. Everybody in the Bible suffered afflictions, turmoil, pearls, imprisonment, setbacks, and defeats to such a degree that we wonder why God has even used them. Faithfully we preach to bring the whole tithe into the storehouse, but the lasting ordinance to observe the Sabbath, to keep it holy, is obsolete.

In the church today, we have offended God. The consequences of our rebellion against God are beyond our understanding. We must see clearly the problem to see clearly the solution. God's anger is real because it is God who has been offended. If Satan could keep us blinded for a little while longer, or keep sin unchecked, then he keeps our testimony to the cross and resurrection which is hurtful to his security.

Six days we shall work, and on the seventh day rest. The Sabbath day is holy. We are not committed to a church, or a denomination, or an organization, but we are committed to Christ. We fight against God the way we behave when it comes to the Sabbath day.

Briefly the Sabbath day is on Saturday. However, because of the resurrection when Jesus rose on the first day of the week, some Christians celebrate on Sunday. The Sabbath day is holy still. Obligation to bring the gospel on the Sabbath is like gathering wood, so be careful.

We are not here to pervert the faith of good Christians. But whosoever does any work on the Sabbath day is to be put to death. Does this sound familiar: "Did God really say...you will not certainly die?" This is the same lie from the foundation of the world. The father of lies is up to the same dirty tricks. Yet we die spiritually. How can a dead church promote living growth?

This is an age of deception, and we cannot pick and choose what scriptures are still legal and binding, because all scriptures are given for reproof and instructions. To honor the Sabbath day is a commandment. It is the law. It is just as important as having no other god before God. The magnitude of this offense cannot be expressed more clearly, because the consequences are beyond our calculation.

From the least to the greatest, all are greedy for gain. Pastors preach what is beneficial or befitting, not wanting any to be offended. Christianity is considered false by the way that scriptures are interpreted and applied. Scripture may differ; therefore, religion tends to practice according to the way interpretation is perceived and understood. False doctrine corrupts the life of the church at its source. Those who rob the church of the gospel deliberately pervert the gospel.

The church is to continue in the apostles' teaching. The apostles were men chosen by God to bear witness of the events of His revelation in Jesus. The teaching is their witness to the physical event of God revealing Himself in Christ, and God is not dishonored by teaching about a fiery place of torment. People think we will return to a state of nonexistence and Satan's deceptive lies would have us believe that God doesn't punish sin, but if we go through life believing that there are no consequences for our sin, then we undermine holiness.

The body of Christian believers has penetrated into the heart of the world in the form of the church. This body makes a deep invasion into the sphere of secular life. Christians are judged, however, by obedience to be not fashioned according to this world. The Christians live in the world and they indulge in worldly activities, but in a different spirit from the world, and this is the church. This body has been separated from sin and the world because God dwells in it with the Holy Spirit. It is the Holy Spirit that seals off the church from the world.

But the Word of God must go forth from the church into all the world. The church is always on the battlefield waging war from within and, from without, struggling to prevent the church from becoming the world. Yet something of the world still lives in the church.

The church needs to stand together against social evils within the body and stand shoulder-to-shoulder against division. Satan is keeping people chained up in spiritual darkness confusing their belief system, weakening their faith with partial truths, and neutralizing their effectiveness. People are becoming greatly dissatisfied with religious leaders and their format on money, appalled by the clergy's emphasis on financial contributions, and many stop attending religious services.

Chapter 10

MODERN DISTRACTIONS!

There is a world empire of false religion. It is a wicked system established on an international plane, which includes both influential organizations and secret societies. The contamination of unclean teaching and practices are incessant.

We have more- or less-relegated religion. It has become a side issue. We take it lightly and leave it for Sunday. The church has cooled down in the Western culture and in the world. People cling to traditional religious forms, but they are not greatly moved by them, nor are they nourished in them, rejecting all religious and moral principles. Touched by the splendor, and power of God has fallen to a notion.

The end has come and stands before us like a silent knight; it waits for the command to reveal itself, for it is hidden in the darkness. Woe to the worthless shepherds who deserted the flock. So I must shepherd the flock marked for slaughter, yet the flock detested me, and the curse was against me. The sword did strike the right eye, and the right eye is totally blinded. These things have tremendous and far-reaching implications. It is better to enter the kingdom of God with one eye than to have two eyes and be thrown into hell.

The church is swayed by men, preoccupied with prosperity, church growth, rapid technological and economic changes. The church let the world dictate the course of their actions making them a part of the world. Different variations of the same truth coming from different angles are often different gospels. People who want a new presentation of the gospel alter the gospel and bring a curse and declare war against God.

Nevertheless, the continuation of the Christian faith has flourished throughout history, even in the midst of enemies and those who have vowed to exterminate the church, and with prayer, devotion, and sacrifice it has continued. Today influence rules. Churches and leaders have confined themselves to groups of people with ethnic political economic and academic likeness; affluence, prestige, power, with all their capabilities and capacity are motivating one another. However, the early church included individuals from every ethnicity, economic, and academic level. This is not true today. Shepherds take care of themselves, full of the world and absorbed in self.

Pastors are dressed to impress in the finest evangelical garb and latest fashions setting trends with a heightened sense of self-importance. Man sits in the pews in a deplorable condition, in a fallen state of moral corruption, while the shepherds are trying to get the most out of life. The things we see, the things that have been done, the church that has been built, you have built on your own that you may consume them upon your own lust. You have fasted for yourselves, you have gone to school for yourselves.

The Lord God did not choose from among seminary graduates those whom He sends out to preach. You heap up teachers to your own liking. Man is now more interested in how the gospel can help *him* in this present life. We are not even a foreshadow of the church as it will be in the future.

We are to reject all that can be seen in exchange for what cannot be seen. Death comes equally to everyone. However, death is not simply the end of us where there is no reward, no punishment, or no consequences. After the resurrection, it was fairly easy for the disciples to set their thoughts on things above; they were not distracted by the worldview around them. The acknowledgment of the advancement of the kingdom of God, the inspiration of His hand moving us forward into the direction of His will, is never seen by the naked eye, but we can see the results.

Break every truce with the world and denounce every compromise with the devil because true faith will produce change. Satan's objective is to have us reject the God of the Bible and choose a new god. Many people turn to Jesus and still don't see any sharper or clearer. The only worldview is a biblical view to see things through God's eyes. Replacing the Lord God has always been the intentions of the adversary Lucifer. The Word of the Lord endures forever, and Satan is determined to prove God wrong that it doesn't. Slowly and meticulously, he perverts and alters the Word of truth to such an abomination that the church surrenders to their changes and are being trampled.

David took the ark of the covenant into the City of Jerusalem. As the ark began to fall, Uzziah touched the ark to steady it, and God struck him dead. We carelessly handle the Word of God, and we are so blind that we cannot see the consequences of our actions. The setup of the abomination seems harmless for those who are unharmed, but for those that are dangerous, words change meanings, and a simple word becomes a wall of rebellion built up for the desolation of the saints.

To desecrate the Word of God with little changes, words that have gone unnoticed or unchallenged, changing words to fit our accurate interpretation. Reaching out to steady the wind. Moving the Word of God through time with our fast-paced society and innovative technologies, looking for a better understanding.

If we violate or forsake the holy covenant, disregard the cost of the blood, desecrate the Sabbath, transgress and break the laws written in our hearts, profane and convert the Word of God to evil use, and violate its sacredness, then we turn away our highest priority. Truce breakers not understanding the operation of the spirit. Never thankful, the imaginations are darkened. Set on the worldview and continue to conform to the world, making a pact with the ruler of this world, and have set the stage for some very serious consequences.

The abomination has slithered onto the scene unnoticed, and the rulers of this world will be successful until the time of wrath is complete. For we do not retain God in our knowledge. There ought to be a people above all other people with a purpose and a mission more important and mighty than any agenda.

Nations against nations, Africa's famines, Japan's earthquakes, and AIDS to Ebola. The hub for religious activity is now the center of violence. Young men lay in the streets with hate for one another, and without a cause they fall dead and deceived. We have preached to the unreached, and now we live in prosperity and peace; we feel secure. Hitler invaded kingdoms when its people felt secure. The curse is upon the church. It is her most difficult hour. The end has come, and the gospel has been preached.

This is not a movement but a move of God. We are prone to think of the elect in this present age as the church, but Israel is God's elect. If we pay close attention to Israel, we will see how tribulation has already begun. The Middle East conflict continues between the two brothers, the Arabs and the Jews, and the birth of the nation of Israel was the start. Russia has a foothold in the Middle East with close ties to Iran. Iran nuclear deal was finalized, and now Jerusalem is a major focus of world conflict. There are war ships in the Middle Eastern waters around the Black Sea, and these are the birth pangs for Israel, the time of Jacob's trouble.

We are already caught completely off guard, and by the time people realize this is the tribulation, it will already be too late. The church's calling is heavenly and not earthly. It is not promised an earthly heritage, but an inheritance incorruptible and undefiled that is reserved in heaven. Nevertheless, the church will be translated before judgment while Israel will be saved through judgment. Yet we are waiting for the Lord to come, but not aware of what His coming involves. Let no man deceive you by any means; one by one as we die in this present age, there are those who are being left behind.

Children, the throne is set, God sits, and the courts are seated; the books are opened. Now let our eyes be opened and watch the spiritual wickedness and demonic forces that hinder our advancement. The church is supposed to be seen as being responsible for inner life, spiritual and moral formation of the world, and we fail. A divided alienated church cannot convert the world to God.

God has never been restricted by human inadequacy or limited by less-than-perfect people. I groan with a bitter broken heart, forced to preach against the church. The donkey just laid down, and Balaam just beat the donkey until it started to speak. The Lord opened my mouth, and we see how guidance comes.

The pews are feeling oppressed by the church because no real and true Christian love is being experienced. The abomination of the unbelieving make superficial confessions of faith in God, while the shepherds' neglect of the gospel leaves the flock ignorant of basic truths. Churches reduce the gospel while millions walk our streets and sit in our pews unchanged. How can we fill our minds with the Word of God when it is constantly changing? Israel rejected God when they wanted a king. We have rejected God by rejecting His Holy Spirit when we ask for a better understanding or interpretation and keep making new translations.

Present-day promises of health and wealth is appealing. They pay tithes, they get what they want, and the soul remains dead. People have exchanged the glorious God for worthless practices. People think they have peace and the sword is at their throat. God judges that which is worthy of being judged. We are responsible and important to God, and our actions have real consequences. The wedding banquet is ready, and we are waiting for the bridegroom to come. Darkness is upon the face of the earth, and a storm is approaching.

We cannot overthrow the purposes of God. We have become completely wicked to the one we most need and the one we most want to hide from. Because we don't see these things, we feel secure. We have made ourselves enemies with rebellion and disobedience, to the one whose laws are broken, whose love is wounded in every sin.

It is hard to distinguish who has gained more power by their wealth as we discern what path to take. People are known for their intelligence and scholastic achievements speculating about the truth, but we do not come with some intellectual speculation.

The apostles came to Jesus privately wanting to know the end of the age or the world as we know it. They did not expect Christ's delay to be prolonged. Two thousand years later, we wait because we will never be able to reverse the effects of what we do to God who is long-suffering, not willing that any should perish.

Chapter 11

REFORMATION WAR

The kingdom of heaven suffers violence! Our modern-day term for violence does not appertain to the violence that takes place in heaven as it does on earth. On earth, violence is increasing with blood shed, and with war, we kill and murder. A fight is physical, and there is the danger of death.

When theologians, scholars, and professors fight, they strive with words, they debate. This is similar to what takes place when there is war in heaven. Satan accuses us, and when our actions are contrary to God's will, we cause him to blaspheme God's holy name. Our war is with words, in prayer, songs, and knowledge of the Scriptures. Jesus defeated Satan with His spoken word. Joshua commanded the people not to shout or make any noise with their voice; neither did a word proceed out of their mouth. Until the appointed time and with a shout of praise, they defeated a whole army.

Our spoken word is very important, and it is to be limited. Everyone has a doctrine, everyone has a revelation, and everyone has an interpretation. Evil communication corrupts, and in everything we do, we use words. There is a very serious element in spoken words that is destructive and at the same time extremely dangerous; don't be ignorant.

Waging spiritual war is praising God more and more, from faith to faith, and strength to strength, praising that word written, or praising that word spoken. Our weapons are mighty through God, pulling down strongholds, casting down imaginations, and bringing every thought into captivity to obedience with a readiness to shout. Our swords are drawn as we march on every page, a war where we shout, and walls fall down. Look at the outward appearance. This world which we clearly see has blinded us so that we cannot see the other side of reality.

We listen to the contemptible speech of the weak, who may be wise but, like the serpent beguiled Eve, turns us from the simplicity of salvation. For the real Christian agenda, families are not to be united in social harmony but torn apart in social disruption because it is not life in this world that matters but life in the world to come. The pleasures of this life are not to be attained but forsaken. Let us fight to enjoy a spiritual union with God. Anything that ties us too closely to this world must be avoided at all cost. This is the lesson of Abraham and Isaac, and this is especially true of the teachings of Jesus Christ.

Who can exercise authority over Christian belief and practice and determine what forms of Christianity is disregarded, set aside, and/or destroyed? A hierarchy of church leaders who could run the church and guarantee its adherence to proper belief and practice, with doctrinal unity. How dangerous is a war where writings are destroyed and forgotten, not reproduced or simply lost? To come together in the church and there be divisions, there must also be heresies, so we thread a thought on the surface and weave a pattern in the core, but through the maze of written words are the instructions.

There was no New Testament, but today, we have twenty-seven books that supports these leaders' vision of the church and their understanding of doctrine ethics and worship by collecting sacred books and assigning them divine status. Everybody who studied the history of early centuries simply accepted the version of these early conflicts. Eventually some scholars questioned the independence of such early Christian leaders.

Confrontations were waged generally on literary grounds, debating over which books to include in the New Testament. However, it was in the fourth century when these leaders gave us the creeds and decided which books would belong to the Scriptures. No one cherished Peter or received his gospel, but someone well-regarded Peter and his gospel, because his sacred text was found buried in the tomb of an Egyptian monk in Egypt four or five hundred years after Serapion had forbidden the gospel's use.

Before Matthew, Mark, Luke, and John the gospel was the gospel of Peter until the bishop asserted his authority and banned its use. These texts and their perspectives look not to the enjoyment of life in the world, but in the things above this world, renunciation of this world, and its pleasures. To disrupt the values of everyday life and its enjoyments, a life apart from the pleasures of the flesh, and in particular sex. For sexual love is not the goal to be achieved, but the pitfall to be avoided. The pleasures of this life are snares to be avoided if we are to experience a spiritual existence with God. It is better to prepare for the coming kingdom, but evangelicals run programs to ensure financial success.

These are texts lost from sight, forgotten, and thought to have been destroyed, buried, or burned. Truth was supposed to be handed down by faithful predecessors who received understanding about God, Christ, the world, and our place in it from the apostles through Jesus. Evidence we consider lost or destroyed, we have been allowed to rediscover.

There were no creeds devised, no doctrinally precise profession, or confession of faith to be recited; just traditional acts of worship, not beliefs. Let us understand that Jesus is the only means of right standing before God, the only way of salvation. We must be right in such a way that everyone else is wrong. For it matters greatly what a person believes now, because our eternal life depends upon it.

The apocalyptic vision of Jesus is lost to most of Christianity. Christian thinking has shifted away from the sense that the world will be destroyed in a future act of divine wrath. These forms of Christianity have been lost and opposed by Christian leaders. We want to hear the gospel of the Savior, not the doctrine of men, because the sayings of Jesus are key to a right relationship with God.

The historical question is, where did we get our New Testament gospel from in the first place, and what parts reveal the truth about what Jesus taught? These texts of Peter both established and helped bring the books of the New Testament into proper perspective. Paul stressed the death and resurrection of Jesus as the way of salvation, but many people have trouble understanding His death as an atonement or accepting the resurrection. Salvation, in essence, comes through saving knowledge. The world is in a cosmic catastrophe, under attack by evil spiritual beings. Life is a matter of spirit, and once we realize that we come from God and He is our ultimate destination, then we will see that this material world is dead and there is no life in it.

Trapped in this material world like a place of confinement, salvation will not be salvation that comes to this world, but it will be salvation from this world. By having proper knowledge, the things that are hidden will be revealed. Must I be the one to disrupt the world's walk of life or the life we have been conformed to, stirring up concerns over the truthfulness of documents?

How can we understand the teachings of Christ if they are not available? Documents, manuscripts, and gospels were lost to future generations, destroyed or forgotten in the struggle to decide what Christians would believe and read. Christians who have established themselves as dominant were determined to establish what future Christians would think about God, Christ, salvation, and the Bible.

There are laws that Jesus clearly indicates did not come from God; for example, the law of divorce which Jesus disallowed by saying, "For your hardness of heart, Moses allowed divorce." The law which indicates that a gift that might benefit one's parents could be donated to the temple instead. This law is from the elders and violates God's commandment to honor your father and mother. Therefore, our views must come from our Savior's teaching founded on one God and followed by the apostolic tradition.

Our views on life, worship, and a relationship with God has been distorted and completely misinterpreted, because it doesn't line up with the will of God. What we believe, what we read, what we do, and the choices we make have significant bearing on who we are and where we are going. How can Christians claim to be heirs of the Jewish scriptures when they do not even keep its laws? The laws of God are meant to induce ethical behavior.

Administrative skills are still important, and we do not oppose those with the proper understanding of the faith and a correct understanding of the truth. However, with Christians doing the best they can to understand and practice what God requires, the belief of one age can still be the deviation of the next.

Appointed leaders of authority are not always right about precious truths of the faith especially when compromising its logic with practical realities. Therefore, we will drop the Trinity title because it is of man. We know that the Father, the Son, and the Holy Spirit are one. God sits on the throne, His Word sits beside Him, and His Holy Spirit stands before Him. Behold He has made His Word His Son, the one through whom God made the world. The intellectual mind trying to work out the mysteries of God stumbles at a true reflection rooted in God, in the form of a human, distinct in person but equal in substance.

The tradition of fights and arguments about writings that have become part of the New Testament have stripped us of rich wisdom. Wars ensued, and many times we ignore the spiritual implications of the battles that we wage on earth. We fight hard drawn-out affairs which keep records and decide how to tell the history of the conflict and keep back knowledge that is needed to bring us wisdom.

We struggle with what we have, and we labor to enter in. We are at a crossroad looking for right beliefs and right ideas in the midst of conflict, theological agendas, and historical accuracy. The competing interpretations of Christianity and the rewritten history of debates are making certain views appear to have been from apostolic times to obscure the real history. But it has not been completely successful, leaving behind traces that can be scrutinized for the truth.

The battle lines are far more blurred. The apostles did not teach the Nicene Creed, Westminster confession, or anything like it. There are so many problems with false understanding of the faith that the infighting is far more intense than we could possibly know, and the false teachers are damnable and far more dangerous today. The church hierarchy with its authority determined what was to be believed, how church affairs were to be conducted, and which books were to be accepted as the scriptural established order.

Think of all those who have departed from this life, while the war of words continues and eternal life is on the line. So it is very important for us to be precise with our understanding. It would be difficult to restructure the world's thinking, living according to our fleshly desires. Nothing can prepare us for the mysteries that have been hidden since the foundation of the world, and this is what makes hell difficult to understand.

The Christian message has become corrupted by foreign elements, altered sometimes beyond recognition. Truth becomes more distant with the passing of time. Meaning of texts in the Bible are not self-evident; however, we have put up so many barriers, rules to interpret a text, and textual constraints on reading that these practices have turned ordinary people who desire to know God away. Men make God inaccessible and off-limits by the walls they build around the knowledge we have and require academic achievement to gain entry.

The literary battles which gave us our New Testament, through manipulation, alterations, inserting, and reinserting words and even sentences to illustrate a point of view, leaving out words; some by accident, some by mistake. Others intentionally alter the sacred texts in different ways but always to the same end of serving their own purposes. Twenty-seven books to the present day, and our New Testament is accepted by Christians.

God has allowed the New Testament, understood to be the Word of God, to work together for our good. We tip our hat to the intelligent scholars, theologians, doctors, and professors whose work is complicated business uncovering the truth about history, sifting through manuscripts, forged documents riddled with alterations, mistakes intentional and accidental in these sacred texts. These are the forerunners destined to assure us that our living is not in vain. These are the real torchbearers.

The four Gospels that made it into the New Testament are all anonymous Christians. The church hierarchy recognized the need for apostolic authorities, and they attributed these books to the apostles. Most scholars today have abandoned these identifications. These books were written by well-educated Greek–speaking and writing Christians. No other books of the New Testament claim to be written by one of Jesus's earthly disciples. Most of the books that came to be included in the New Testament are not apostolic.

There are those who update the Bible once a year, literally tampering with the wording of documents held to be sacred to make them say what they want them to say. To compromise with the changing times, they have become in all honesty changes for easy reading, deceptive changes reproduced in most of our English Bibles.

All forms of modern Christianity go back to one form or another, and because of this, on the bookshelves in virtually every home is the Bible. Ever wonder and contemplate the life of the apostles after the resurrection, where no record is available for us? It was the scholars in the modern period who began to rediscover the covered-over or hidden secret writings. What we don't know is what was lost, destroyed, or hidden, what was covered that was truth, denounced, or forgotten in this war. Because it is a fearful thing to live in vain with uncertain steps toward eternity.

Death reigned from Adam to Moses, two thousand years; from Moses to Christ, two thousand years; and from Christ to us today, two thousand years. This is the seventh day. No more floods and public acts, the work is finished. God's way of dealing with sin is complete. Did we miss the molecular structure of those glorified bodies that was not disturbed as they passed through solid objects? Because the Holy Spirit will cease to be felt through the true church as we wait for the rapture.

We are not looking for a sign but listening for a sound, the last trump—the shout, the voice of the archangel, and the trump of God. God of heaven set up a kingdom which shall never be destroyed, and the kingdom was not left to other people, yet other people seem to have taken control of a kingdom that they thought was abandoned.

Having set up a democracy dictatorship, which is a system by the people, that are appointing leaders to their liking governed and overbearing with its absolute authority, many people credit themselves with righteous living and refuse to expose themselves. They rationalize themselves by their works and lift up holy hands to declare themselves clean.

Reach deep into thought as our mind's eye takes us to the ancient days of Noah, being reminded by the episode as if we were in attendance. For the evidence of this incident is clearly seen being understood by the things that are made. For we see the rainbow as the covenant symbol and the breaking up of the earth's surface as the evidence. The worn paths from the work that must be done, the labor, and long days of an un-relentless task to make an ark of gopher wood three stories high.

Not one person offered to lend Noah a hand, especially when men thought they were not going to get paid. But to help build the ark and run under its shelter for protection spares a life and is enough payment. Is not life more precious than the pleasures? Today evidence proves that we behave in the exact same manner as in the days of Noah, and even worse.

Cutting wood and carrying wood, logging is still a tough job, and without modern-day equipment, more so. A deadline is looming even as in the days of Noah, no law had been given, and today we live like no law exists. Every thought is only evil continually. Howl, for the day of the Lord is at hand. It shall come as destruction from the Almighty. All flesh has corrupted his way upon the earth. The same wickedness of man is the same wickedness that was found in Satan.

This is why God destroyed all flesh with a flood of water, and that wickedness is found in us again. The days are evil, people are greedy of gain. God first saw us by our thoughts and judged us by them. If every imagination of thought is evil, then what are we thinking? Eating, drinking, and living it up while man is building the ark. Dragging wood, measuring, cutting, tying, strengthening, and binding. The onlookers and giants stare. We are the public spectacles, praying, fasting, reading, preaching, and teaching. The law comes from the evil that men do, to help our defective sight. For God looked upon the earth, and it repented Him that He had made us.

They were cutting themselves, in their flesh for the dead, printing marks upon their bodies, much of the same things that we do today with tattoos. Marking the skin in patterns and sometimes for the dead. Paving the way for the mark of the beast to be put on our hands or in our forehead, piercing the skin as wickedness grows with each passing moment. If these things had come before God to end all flesh, then why do we still not see how easy it is to offend God? A people without the law by their wicked thoughts and violent behavior died, and we behave worst.

So as the days of Noah, with the world greatly advanced and filled with violence, murder, wars, destruction, and death, with no relationship with God nor any knowledge, blind and ignorant, we run and rebel at the work He has called us to do. Every sort does not come to the call to be kept alive. The earth is filled with violence again, and we should expect nothing less than fire, and we are not terrified. That wicked generation refused to believe the truth, and finally the flood came and took them all away.

So Noah builds, and the laborers are few. There are lots of idle people standing around watching in unbelief as Noah builds the ark with no help. While the world is enjoying the pleasures of this life, things continue unchanged and events of important spiritual significance are going unnoticed. But as in the days of Noah, where it took Noah approximately one hundred years to build the ark, God has given us all of our life to get on board. But we are walking pass what God is building and ignoring what God is doing.

In the days of Noah, people were marrying and being given into marriage; today people are marrying and being given into same-sex marriages. The human history had a beginning, and it will have an end according to God who brought it into existence. Let us walk as if the next step will carry us across the threshold of heaven.

The sin bearer became accursed of God, forsaken of God, crushed under the weight of God's wrath. His death paid the debt for sin, satisfied the demands of God's justice, and appeased His wrath. God is just, and the guilty cannot be pardoned until the demands of His laws are satisfied. Jesus received the sour wine, and He said,

"It is finished." After that He had provided cleansing for sins. He sat down.

Christ was made sin the same way believers become the righteousness of God. As a result of the work of Christ on our behalf, we are considered righteous before God. Guilty before the judgment seat of God, in our place, God considered Him guilty of our crimes and treated Him with the judgment we deserved. It was real guilt bringing real anguish to His soul. He stood in our place, bored our sins, carried our guilt, and experienced the full measure of the wrath of God. And now it is finished. It is finished, and now God sits in His holy hill and waits to see who will put forth His hand and take from the tree of life. Who will believe our report?

If any religious faith concludes that God is a loving God and He doesn't punish people and doubt the righteous judgment of God, then they need only to look to the cross. The victory chant for entrance into Christianity is the resurrection; this is the gospel's power. Christ was raised from the dead; this was the final act. The resurrection of Christ establishes evidence that His work on our behalf has been completed.

Modern-day technology excavations and discoveries bring us to our present day. People have spent years searching for the truth to know God. It is almost impossible to study God because all we have is nature, while man fights over the right of way to God's Word. Men have been so intelligent in gathering the truth, and people still ignore the evidence. The minds of people have been enslaved with a false sense of direction, after we have found key discoveries that propels us to this understanding.

Why is this knowledge so important, that it would cause certain people to believe that they are the only ones allowed to administer it, and have convinced the world of its infallible teaching? We are taught that the Word of God is infallible, but man wrote the word and we are not infallible. But we have an infallible Word of God that no one is able to alter, touch, translate, interpret, or administer. These are the orders handed down by those who wrote it, those who could change it, rewrite it, kill and confine because of it. Those who have total authority over it finally to release it, and it has no power whatsoever.

Partial truth is a lie, and if people do not write like this and inform Christians around the world about the truth, it is because they understand how many people believe in the Bible. It is up to the Christian to search for the truth, and there are many useful resources to help a person gather the truth. But people should not be left with a false sense of direction, and we are not to withhold corn from the people.

When the apostles, who were appointed by God and moved by the Holy Spirit, first spoke the Word, rest assure that it was done in simplicity. The speaker was not speaking in code to confuse their audience especially if they were determining to impart faith in Christ. We find that the "book of love," no matter how many beautiful self-guiding stories it has, has a simple message of love and faith.

Doctrinal exactitude for good conduct living is a great control measure, but a real life-changing experience comes from a revelation that is not controlled by men. However, people disregard revelations. Even the Holy Spirit will not impart complex theory to a person of faith. We have been given a complex guide to faith, God, and salvation instead of the simplicity of love.

About the Author

A revelation from God! When God is speaking, He is using the same vehicles of communication He has used for the past six thousand years—men of low degree, men of low status, wisdom that makes foolish the wisdom of men.

Tuck takes the two-thousand-year-old Christian history, interprets complex language of scholars, uncovers important biblical truths left behind, and addresses complex debates and important religious doctrines.

Tuck is a man who God has taken seriously because he has taken the eternal Word seriously, rekindling the Reformation that Luther or Calvin never finished.

Rulers and leaders, scholars and professors who stumbled at the Bible's most elusive truths, conjured up false doctrines and passed them on as God's words, truth hidden under an intellectual structure of words, which led to intense and bitter debates.

Tuck weaves into this nonfiction narrative a Reformation with historical facts addressing these complex debates. Tuck is professor and a scholar ordained by God who has studied the Bible from his youth and has studied under the inspiration of the Holy Spirit.

The Book on the Shelf of Love is a sound, a trumpet that can be read as a completion of God's Word, silencing these debates for the last warning.

Tuck delivers more than a story. It can be described as a literal word of God. This book is a sound, an alarm to the entire world addressing readers with both a general and scholarly interest.